Praise for Jules Brown's books

'The best kind of travel companion – funny, informed and always up for an adventure.'
Martin Dunford, Rough Guides founder

'I laughed out aloud so much that I scared the cat!'
Amazon reviewer (5 stars)

'This is the kind of travel writing I love – full of charming moments, unusual sights and a writer who is determined to discover what really makes a place unique.'
Amazon reviewer (5 stars)

'A very funny travel writer … I highly recommend this journey.'
Edie Jarolim, author of *Getting Naked for Money*

'Brown is not only a great traveller, he's a brilliant storyteller … This is travel writing at its best.'
Heidi Slowinski, US book reviewer

'I feel I have been travelling … with a new, entertainingly witty friend.'
Sue Bavey, UK book reviewer

Contents

Introduction

I ONCE WENT on a hiking tour deep in the Borneo jungle with an ex-army Malay tracker who claimed his name was Winston. Apart from that, I saw no reason to doubt him about anything, because within about ten minutes he'd hacked his way through the undergrowth with a fearsome machete, shown us some monkeys and stopped us toppling off a hidden rock ledge to certain doom.

At some point we stopped at a clearing in the trees for a breather. Winston dropped to his haunches and crouched among the leaf litter. Resting on decayed, fallen logs and leaning against soaring, creeper-clad trunks, we listened while Winston told us about the jungle wildlife – the snakes, the giant spiders, the fire ants that cause anaphylactic shock, the rainforest stick insects the length of your forearm, the pincer-clawed beetles, the burrowing wasps.

"So what's the best tip, Winston," someone said, "you know, to stay safe in the jungle?"

"Never lean on a tree," said Winston, at which half the group leapt in the air, shaking fire ants out of their hair.

"Or sit on a dead tree trunk," he added, which was the cue for the other half to spring upright, dusting plate-sized spiders off their behinds.

I often think of Winston when people ask me for travel tips.

I don't mind being asked. I'm a travel writer, it's all part of the job. But I'm never sure how much help I'm going to be. If you want a steer on the latest hot restaurants in Barcelona, you'll get more useful advice from TripAdvisor these days than from me. Also, the kind of travelling I do now – basically pottering about in random bits of assorted countries, pleasing myself – doesn't really lend itself to assembling a list of must-see destinations or recommended hotels.

But, like Winston, I do have some travel tips that might come in useful in certain situations. Don't order the chicken; keep the sea on your right; listen to the nice policeman; try not to be sick in your face-mask – there are times when I guarantee that these hard-won pieces of advice will help you on your travels. And I shouldn't have to say it, but you did ask – never pack an ice-axe.

A hitch in time in Spain

A BIT LIKE Withnail in the film, who went "on holiday by mistake," I became a traveller by accident.

Two years out of college, in 1985, I was living in London and working in an office, because that's what I thought you had to do.

I rode in every morning on the bus and spent the day compiling reports for the Greater London Council about installing pedestrian crossings on busy roads. This was exactly as exciting as it sounds. It largely involved reading technical digests from traffic engineers who had come up with cunning plans to stop people getting run over in central London. I then wrote letters in longhand to the Ambulance Service and the Fire Brigade asking what they thought about our latest wheeze to install a pedestrian crossing somewhere. I sent the letters to be typed up in Secretarial Services, which was a frightening room in a different building staffed by bold and assertive women with lightning fingers whose sole other duty was to terrorise know-nothing college boys. They took their job very seriously and did it very well.

After about a month, letters would arrive back from the Ambulance Service and the Fire Brigade saying that, on the whole and taken in the round, in principle and without prejudice, they had no objection to my plan to prevent people from being mown down on the capital's highways. I punched holes in the letters, placed them in manila folders, and then wrote a report for the Transport Committee, recommending the installation of the pedestrian crossing, given the wholehearted support of our tremendous emergency services. I never quite understood what the Ambulance Service and Fire Brigade had to do with it all, but assumed the whole thing was on a strictly need-to-know basis.

It goes without saying that I didn't want to do this job for the rest of my life. Then again, I was twenty-three and didn't know anything about anything. Plus, I got paid quite a lot to do not very much in a waterside office that overlooked the River Thames and the Houses of Parliament. On sunny days, that seemed like quite the stroke of luck.

It would be convenient to say that I daydreamed at my desk about seeing the world, but the truth is that we filled in the morning hours with Office Olympics – chair-racing, desk ping-pong, bin-ball and elastic-band-shooting were our specialist sports. There were phones on our desks that never rang but which could be used to dial premium-rate call-lines for football reports, radio station competitions and, on one memorable and presumably hugely expensive occasion, the live feed from a NASA spacecraft launch in Florida. We wasted another hour or two a day shambling between sandwich shop and coffee machine, went to the subsidised works' bar at lunchtime, cleared off home at the stroke of four and spent most nights in the pub. Not-really-work, drink, sleep, bus, repeat. Some of those pedestrian crossings are doubtless still there, though not necessarily in the right street or with the correct authorisations.

Then one day I bought a book called the *Hitch-hiker's Guide to Europe* – long out of print now but, at the time, considered a reasonable purchase for anyone considering going travelling. It had first been published in 1971, so the hippy-trail ethos behind it – showing you how to get around and across Europe as cheaply as possible – was well established. It reflected a growing interest in travelling the world on a budget: the first Lonely Planet guide was published in 1975; Rough Guides followed in 1982.

I'd done some hitch-hiking at college to save money on bus and train fares, but it hadn't struck me as a lifestyle I might choose, rather a means of making more money available for beer. I wasn't really thinking of travelling anywhere either, but the book seemed like a fun thing to read between naps at work.

Now, in its defence, I honestly think that the *Hitch-hiker's Guide to Europe* must have inspired me to quit my job and head off abroad. I don't have any evidence of that, and I can't remember a particular moment of inspiration, but it seems to be the case that before I read the book I had no intention of going anywhere and after I read it I left my job and bought a backpack. Within a couple of months, I was on the ferry from the UK to Spain.

However, that can't be right, because even a cursory reading of the book showed it to be largely bonkers.

Partly it was a product of its time and its author, who I imagine was – again with no evidence – a beardy gent in sandals who knew his way around a kaftan. Suggested budgets had a daily allowance for cigarettes and one heading was "Basic rules to follow when making a black-market currency deal." The guide assumed you were carrying drugs – how could you not be? – and considerately warned readers of the old "hippy-type spy gimmick" in Italy where buying dope from an undercover narc could get you three years in the slammer.

Quite apart from fourteen pages devoted to "How to hitch" – not just 'stick your thumb out by the side of the road' then – there were endless money-saving and survival tips, which at least started off sensibly. Take a tent, get a youth hostel card, wear a money-belt – these still seem like sound plans today for a young traveller. But quicker than you could say hippy-type spy gimmick, the *Hitch-hiker's Guide to Europe* started suggesting things that – even in the 1970s and 1980s – surely can't have been good ideas, however keen you were to stay on the road.

Selling your blood, for example. The guide was very big on that. Didn't seem to think it was in any way crazy as long as you – *shudders while reading today* – checked the needle was clean and didn't let them take more than half a litre. You – the medically unqualified hitch-hiker – had to do the checking, obviously. Not the struck-off doctor in the backwoods hospital in an unspecified country willing to drain the blood from impecunious backpackers; they'd bleed you dry with a dirty needle soon as look at you, was the implication.

Other ideas championed by the guide, in ascending order of WTF-ery, were: buying duty-free cigarettes to take from Spain to Denmark to sell in the street; sleeping in a church or construction site; and asking to spend the night in the local police cell. Meanwhile, in the glorious markets of Europe you were urged to check the floors for edible wastage, cut out the bad bits and tuck in.

Restaurants were largely a no-go for the impoverished hitch-hiker, though there was one top tip – and this was my favourite bit in the entire book. Chinese restaurants, it was pointed out, always serve boiled rice, so there's nothing to stop you going in, ordering a bowl and eating it with the free soy sauce provided. Nothing at all, except, well, you know, all the obvious things. Enter hairy backpacker, muddied from a night in a cement mixer, pockets full of contraband fags, who nonchalantly peruses the menu and decides that, while it all sounds very nice, what he really wants is a single bowl of plain rice. And will Sir be requiring anything else? No, very good Sir. More soy sauce? Certainly Sir.

If that fanciful scenario never played out, neither presumably did the one involving the ultimate, last-resort, end-of-the-line suggestion of pawning your boots, or even your rucksack. The genius behind the guide didn't make it entirely clear how you were supposed to carry on hitch-hiking after that ("Bundle your stuff into something else" was the best that they could come up with).

As if this delightful confection of nonsense wasn't enough, readers of the guide were encouraged to write in with their own budget travel tips, which were then printed to help others. They can't all have been messing with the author – some of them must have been serious – but it's genuinely hard to tell. One guy claimed to have found a chair on a rubbish tip, hitched into town with the chair and then sold it to a junk shop. Another person's big idea was to pick flowers in city parks in the dead of night and then sell them on the street during the day. Let us just count the many ways for that idea to go badly wrong, mostly involving muggers, drug-dealers and police truncheons. My favourite suggestion, though, was a top packing tip for campers, which was that instead of taking a plastic plate, you were advised to pack a frisbee: handy and plate-shaped, obviously, but also useful for roadside games between lifts.

All this rather joyful crazy talk was, I repeat, printed in a conventionally published paperback by a mainstream publisher. A book that I read and apparently then thought, "Europe, here I come, where's my frisbee?"

I fixed on Portugal as my destination – for reasons lost in the mists of time – and bought the first edition of the *Rough Guide to Portugal*, which had just come out. This was noticeably less mad and more useful than the *Hitch-hiker's Guide to Europe*, which covered the entire country of Portugal in five scant pages. Top hitch-hiker's tip? Hang out with the fishermen on the Algarve, who will give you free fish to sell on yourself. I am not making this up.

The *Rough Guide*, on the other hand, presented Portugal as a fascinating country of gentle ways, historic sights, bucolic towns, pristine beaches and cheap prices; the sort of place you could fall in love with. It proved to be so and, later, when I ended up working for Rough Guides, I covered Portugal for them as a writer for over twenty-five years.

But that was in my unseen future. Back then, all I knew was that Portugal was *there* and I was *here*, with the sea, France and Spain in between. The *Hitch-hiker's Guide* would have me thumb all the way – two thousand kilometres, Calais to Porto – living off pockets full of mashed potato and sleeping in the doorways of football stadiums (only one of those tips was not actually in the book … go on, have a guess). The *Rough Guide to Portugal* suggested the more sensible overnight ferry from Plymouth on England's south coast to Santander on Spain's north coast, from where it was a far more reasonable three hundred and fifty kilometres to the Portuguese border. That seemed like a hitchable distance, even for a novice.

I financed the trip by cashing in the two years' worth of contributions I'd made to my Council pension, which amounted to about a thousand quid. To any twenty-three year old reading this, obviously don't do that. If I'd left the money there until retirement, I'd be living on my yacht in the Caribbean by now – investing in a gold-plated, local-authority, final-salary pension scheme being a bit like having put a hundred pounds into Amazon as a start-up and forgetting all about it until someone turns up at your door with one of those out-sized cardboard cheques and a banner that says "Winner!"

Equally, I was twenty-three. Pensions. Don't be ridiculous, where do I sign?

Now all that was left was the packing and, thankfully, the *Hitch-hiker's Guide to Europe* had plenty to say on the subject, not all of it insane.

Let's take the backpack, clothes and walking boots as read. I could use them as advertised or sell them to a pawn shop, whichever suited. Other things on the list were a sleeping bag, foam mat, plastic bivouac bag, water bottle, aspirin, insect repellent, blister plasters and antiseptic cream – they all seemed fairly reasonable suggestions.

On toiletries, the guide and I differed. It suggested "using other people's soap where possible" and taking lots of loo paper because "most toilets on the Continent" didn't have any. As it was becoming clear that the right thing to do in any given circumstance was ask what the *Hitch-hiker's Guide* recommended and then do the opposite, I packed my own soap and trusted the entire continent of Europe, forty-four countries, to have some bog roll.

I wish now – and wished then, fairly shortly after leaving – that I hadn't listened to the guide when it came to packing and carrying cooking gear. Thinking I'd be saving money by sleeping out in the wild and foraging in market bins, I packed a portable gas stove, a spare gas canister, a box of matches, a spare box of matches, two canteen sets, a plastic plate, bowl and mug, cutlery, a small kitchen knife, bottle- and can-opener, hip flask, water-purification tablets, and even some little, portable, plastic salt and pepper pots.

Oh, how I laughed when I finally got to Spain – crushed by the weight of my pack – to discover that a bed for the night cost a couple of quid and a full meal ran to under a pound. The first time I ever stood in a Spanish bar, the guy poured me a glass of red wine from a barrel above his head and charged me seven English pence. I nearly wept. What's more, the recommended water-purification tablets turned out to be useless on account of it being 1985 and not 1885: you could drink the water straight out of the taps. They even put pepper and salt on the tables for the customers in Spain; no need to have brought my own.

I could at least blame the *Hitch-hiker's Guide* for most of the above. However, the last items stuffed in the mighty backpack were all my fault. A pair of scissors. No idea – scrapbooking on the road? Needle and thread, clothes pegs, cloth patches and a small ball of string – I clearly thought I was going on holiday to the fourteenth century. And finally, reading material and music.

Look, it was the 1980s. Today you'd just have your phone. I packed the latest technology, namely a Walkman, a pair of headphones and a zip-up case of mix-tapes, which took up a lot of room.

By now the pack resembled the Leaning Tower of Human and weighed about a ton, so there wasn't a great deal of space left, which meant that the obvious choice for a book was that slender essay, *Ulysses*, by James Joyce. To be fair, it's only one sentence long; it's just that the sentence goes on for about a thousand impenetrable pages. I admire my young-brain logic. The book no one can read or enjoy was certainly going to last me many months. But it was the size and weight of three bricks.

Even the *Hitch-hiker's Guide to Europe*, in all its barking glory, didn't recommend taking a hefty, experimental, modernist novel along for the ride.

But there we were, I'd quit my job and the packing was done. There really was nothing else for it now but to start to become a hitch-hiker.

I caught the ferry from Plymouth to Santander on the twenty-sixth of August, 1985. I know that because I kept a diary at the time and, looking at it now, it's hard to read because it's mortifyingly bad. I was barely a traveller, I hadn't yet hitch-hiked anywhere, and I definitely wasn't a writer. I mean, don't get me wrong, I wrote – God, how I wrote, page after page of self-absorbed drivel; I must have done nothing else on that boat for the entire twenty-four-hour trip. Sample passages – "After two years enmeshed in London's social snares ..." or "My confidence ebbed with the tide as I watched the shores of England recede in the distance." I used the words tenet, engendered, besuited, vicarious, eventualities and pragmatist. I described time as "the tripping hours" and shadowy figures on deck as invisible to "the night-deceived eye."

I know, what can I say? I was twenty-three, I had a degree and knew a lot of words, but I couldn't write for toffee. I'd be fine in the future, once I'd had my copy knocked about by gnarly editors, and once I had something to write about. But at the time I didn't know any of that, so I bashed out some more dreadfully verbose notes, agonised a bit about my soul and my emotions, and then went to see *Starman* at the ship's cinema.

The next morning dawned fair – sorry, diary again – and we edged slowly into Santander. If ever there was an inspirational, formative experience, that was one. Thinking about it now still makes the hairs stand up on the back of my neck – the ship slipping into port as the sun rose over the old town, lighting up the sweeping bay beyond. If there's any better way to arrive in a new place than by sea at dawn, I'd like to know about it.

As I stood at the rail on deck watching Spain – and travel – approach, I had the good fortune to strike up a conversation with a South African couple, Sue and Pete. They had a beat-up old car which they assured me was going to get them to Lisbon. Would I like a lift?

Three-hundred-and-four pages of the *Hitch-hiker's Guide to Europe* and not once, anywhere, did it say that I'd get offered a lift on a boat. Not only that, but a single lift all the way to Portugal, without having to employ any of the ludicrous hitching schemes and plans dreamt up by the loonies who wrote into the *Hitch-hiker's Guide*. (Pray to cars on your knees; hold up a sign saying "I wash"; and, best of all, hide your ice-axe to increase your chances of a lift. Ice-axe, yes. Like that's something you would genuinely take with you and, in the normal course of events, have attached to the outside of your backpack, because that wouldn't freak out any of the locals at all in, say, Madrid, as you tramped around the Plaza Mayor with a razor-pointed axe. The border guards, the police, they've all been fine with the ice-axe by the way, waved it straight on through, It's just the passing motorists we're having to hide it from. So, no ice-axe then, got it. The book really was the gift that kept on giving.)

I did want a lift as it happened, Pete and Sue. Those fourteen pages on "How to hitch"? Not required. I could use them for toilet paper on the tissue-deprived Continent.

I don't recall anything about my new friends – the diary is strangely silent – although I did write down something that Sue said as we barrelled through the Cantabrian countryside in their tightly packed car. That something made me think I wasn't yet ready to be a proper traveller and hitch-hiker.

"What I love about all this," she said, gesturing at middle-of-nowhere Spain, "is the fact that I just don't know where I'll be sleeping tonight."

To be honest, that was what was worrying me. I didn't love that at all. I was starting to get nervous at the prospect of striking out alone. It was dawning on me that "travelling" meant that I had to travel somewhere I hadn't been before, where I didn't know what to do, and where I didn't speak the language.

Which is what makes what happened next so baffling.

"Let me out here," I said, as we approached Burgos, a couple of hours' drive south of Santander.

The pair of them were heading for Madrid and then Lisbon, and I could have stayed in the car and known exactly where I was sleeping that night. With them, wherever they decided, I wasn't fussy. Budge up Sue and Pete, the double bed's fine with me.

But I had the *Rough Guide* and I had my plans, which involved starting at the top end of Portugal and working my way down. Burgos was within striking distance of Zamora and the northern Portuguese border, so they dropped me off on the outskirts of a town I'd never heard of and left me to it.

It took me another week to get from Burgos to Portugal but that's another story. There and then, I had Spain to deal with, which seemed quite impossible – carrying a ludicrously heavy backpack, speaking no Spanish, advised by a guidebook whose entire entry for Burgos ran to six words ("home of the legendary El Cid"). I was no expert, but I didn't see how that nugget of information would help with the more pressing matters of finding out where I was and what I was supposed to do next.

In the end, it was surprisingly easy. Sue and Pete would have been proud of me.

I followed the cars in the direction marked "Centro," spotted another sign that said "Turismo" and then another that said "Hotel," and I was up and running with this whole travelling business. I stood in the foyer of a cheap-looking pension, where a bemused owner watched me unpacking water-purification tablets, cotton thread, corkscrews and salt and pepper shakers as I searched for my passport. I was shown to a room with a lumpy bed, a noisy ceiling fan and a window that looked out over an internal courtyard of potted plants and clothes lines. Looked like I wasn't going to need the sleeping bag or bivouac bag then, but there was still time for the clothes pegs to come in handy.

Later, I walked through a monumental gateway into a medieval old town dominated by a glorious cathedral, where –

had I but known – I could have inspected the tomb of the legendary El Cid. I stumbled into a bar full of old men in a back alley where I thought I must have misheard the price of a glass of wine, and I finished the night eating in a local restaurant and not fishing mildewed cabbages out of a market bin.

Burgos by mistake, without so much as having to put my thumb out. That was the place I became a traveller.

A cruise along the edge in Norway

MY FAULT REALLY. I should have looked at the map. Rookie mistake.

When Rough Guides said "Norway?", I said "great!", thinking that Oslo wouldn't be that hard to get to. It turned out that there was a bit more to it than that, but there were trains and buses that went to all the southern towns, and ferries that zipped around the western fjords. I exhausted all the bits of Norway I'd heard of in about a month and wrote a first draft of the first edition of the *Rough Guide to Scandinavia* that was pretty enthusiastic under the circumstances – those being that I'd had to survive in hostel dorms, eating nothing but rye crackers and shrimp paste for several weeks while backpacking around Europe's most notoriously expensive country. (At least I ate the local produce. My co-author, sent at the same time to Finland, packed enough peanut-butter sandwiches to last him a week in Helsinki. I'm not sure his wasn't the better idea.)

When Rough Guides inspected my work and said "Where's the rest of it?", I said "Hang on, bear with" and took a closer look at the map.

I'm not going to lie, there's quite a bit of Norway that I hadn't thought I'd need to go to. On account of the "Well, why would you?" rejoinder when someone asks, "Have you ever been to Mo i Rana, an industrial town dominated by an enormous steel plant?"

It seemed, on investigation, that Mo i Rana was only the half of it. There were distant towns with *Lord of the Rings*-style names such as Bodø and Narvik – the latter was a cool fourteen hundred kilometres from Oslo – whose attractions were also heavily biased on the engineering and industrial side of things. Fish-processing also seemed to be big in the region, ditto iron-ore mining. Tromsø, with its Arctic cathedral, appeared more promising, based on the notion that it was also known locally as the "Paris of the North." This, I thought, I have to see. My future guidebook readers would surely expect coverage of a hitherto unknown croissant-cheese-and-jazz hold-out somewhere north of the Arctic Circle.

The more I looked, the more challenging the job seemed. North of Trondheim – the country's third-biggest city, and about the furthest place I'd been so far – Norway narrows and stretches, uncurling in a slender finger that hugs the top of Sweden and extends all the way east to the Russian border. It goes on and on, and even when you get as far as the Gallic delights of Tromsø there are still another eight hundred kilometres to go until you reach the town of Kirkenes, which is the very last place you can go in Norway.

Whether anyone would want to go to Kirkenes was, apparently, beside the point. Rough Guides were nothing if not comprehensive and my assignment was to deliver a full and complete guide to Norway, however ridiculously remote the destination. I had to go to Kirkenes and all points in between and, because this was the 1980s, I couldn't just stay at home and copy it off Wikipedia.

Rough Guides had a sweetener though. Through some deal with the Norwegian Tourist Board they had secured me a ticket for what was billed as a cruise, and which I continued to believe was an actual cruise until I turned up at Bergen to catch the boat. I was a foolish young travel writer; I'd spent all my research money on rye crackers and shrimp paste. Of course I believed I had a berth on a cruise boat, rum punch on the Captain's table and all.

I should have known. After all, these were the people who were advertising Tromsø as the Paris of the North.

What I was actually boarding was the *Hurtigruten* – or "express route" – a coastal shipping service that ran from Bergen along the western and northern coast of Norway as far as my old friend Kirkenes – a twelve-day, two-thousand-four-hundred-kilometre round-trip with stops in thirty-four ports, at least thirty of which I'd never heard of. Nonetheless, a cruise is a cruise. Show me my cabin, I thought. Point the way to the pool and quoits deck. Stick me down for the cabaret and midnight buffet.

The good news was that my ticket was valid for a free return trip as far as Kirkenes. As for the rest, I could dream on.

Historically, the route had been a lifeline for some of the most isolated communities in mainland Europe, with daily ships running north and south along the Norwegian coast since the 1890s. My source of information was an ancient Baedeker's guide to Norway, on wafer-thin paper and bound in red leather, which talked of the reliability and excellence of the service in the early days of the twentieth century. Most of northern Norway still didn't have proper roads or railway tracks until well after World War II, so there was no irony intended by the name – even though it took several days, the "express route" really was the fastest way to reach the farthest flung parts of the country.

The ships had been upgraded over the years – the very first were steamers – but they were working vessels, as a glance at the cargo cranes on deck confirmed, and still the only transport and freight link to many small towns. There were even cabins on board. It's just that I didn't have one. Tourist board largesse only extended so far. I could sleep on a cushion in the lounge if I wanted, or I could get off at whichever port we called at, spend the night in a draughty seamen's hostel and re-join the service the next day.

There weren't any other contemporary guidebooks to Norway to give me a clue as to what was to come, and the Baedeker guide (1911 edition) was no help at all, beyond solid entertainment value. For instance, of northern Norway, it had this to say: "It possesses attractions for the scientific traveller and the sportsman, but can hardly be recommended for the ordinary tourist." I think they must have meant me.

I did have some idea what to expect though, thanks to the brochure I managed to snaffle from Bergen's tourist office, and it all sounded rather thrilling. For a start, I was going to cross the Arctic Circle into the Land of the Midnight Sun – just after the undoubted tourist hotspot of Mo i Rana, as it happened, en route to the port at Bodø. There were going to be fjords and fishing villages, mountains and waterfalls, shining waters and sea glaciers, and small harbours and swirling mists on what the brochure was calling the most beautiful sea voyage in the world. The word "majestic" was bandied about a lot and there were glossy images of smiling people in chunky knitwear eating alarmingly large king crabs on lobster-pot-filled harboursides.

The reality was slightly different for a travel writer on a budget, trying to make the most of free transport around the northern extremities of Europe. My food allowance for a start was at the cheese-and-crackers end of the spectrum and I never once had a beer during my whole time in Norway because that would have meant taking out a loan or selling a kidney. I got off the boat when I could, but if I'm strictly honest, I'd have to say that some of the accounts I wrote of northern Norwegian towns were based on the sketchiest of visits. When the choice was between paying for a night's overpriced accommodation – and spending twenty-four long hours – in the Norse equivalent of Middlesbrough (insert your own unlikely domestic tourist destination) or stepping off the ship for an hour or two while they unloaded cargo, I unfailingly chose the latter.

Take Hammerfest. Excellent name and with the undoubted draw of being the world's most northerly town with over ten thousand inhabitants (you can hear the bold claim creaking in the caveat). Also, the first town in Europe to have its streets lit by electric light. Two reasons, you would have thought, for a travel writer to spend as much time as possible investigating its culture and nightlife. And yet … Hammerfest was burned to the ground in 1890, rebuilt, destroyed again by retreating German forces at the end of World War II, and then rebuilt again as a fish-processing site and natural-gas port. Consequently, I didn't feel that bad about skipping round for an hour or so, going "Nope, nothing much to see here" and getting back on board. I was even validated by no less a travel writer than Bill Bryson who came here in search of the Northern Lights and wrote of Hammerfest as "an agreeable enough town in a thank-you-God-for-not-making-me-live-here sort of way." Bill comes from Des Moines, Iowa; I come from Huddersfield, West Yorkshire. We both know what we're talking about.

I did stop properly at the next port, Honningsvåg, which at the time was involved in an unseemly dispute about which was the most northerly town in the world. Hammerfest, as we've seen, was making the claim for itself and pointing out that Honningsvåg was only a village. Honningsvåg was saying nuts to that, we're actually further north than you (true) and size doesn't matter (erm). This was resolved well after my visit, in 1996, when Honningsvåg was granted town status – so now they are both holders of the title, "The most northerly town in the world," one under ten thousand inhabitants and one over, which seems like an entirely Scandinavian compromise if ever I've heard one.

Anyway, that was not at all why I thought I'd spend some of my valuable time and money in a place I later described as "in the middle of a treeless, windswept terrain, surrounded by snow fences to protect it from avalanches." Charming as it sounds, I was instead intent on reaching Nordkapp, the North Cape – the northernmost accessible point of mainland Europe – which had been a pilgrimage site for over three hundred years, and an indigenous sacrificial site long before that. The *Hurtigruten* ships sail around the Cape when the inland roads are blocked by snow, giving you a view of Nordkapp from the sea. But in summer you can reach the Cape by land, riding the last thirty-four kilometres by bus from Honningsvåg, along a winding plateau road where herds of reindeer graze and snow patches still hug the hillside in July.

I ended up walking and hitching some of the way there, to an isolated clifftop with – surprise, surprise – only an arguable claim to being the northernmost point in Europe. There's always someone that wants to make a fuss, in this case another mainland cliff that is technically further north but doesn't have a road going to it. So Nordkapp still gets the kudos, but whether it's the absolute northernmost point of Europe or not doesn't really matter, as there is something about this bleak, wind-battered promontory on the edge of a continent that makes the journey fully worthwhile. Standing on the plateau, I was three hundred metres above the icy Arctic Ocean, with only the distant Svalbard archipelago to the north between me and the North Pole. Later, at home, I dredged up a quotation by a seventeenth-century traveller, Francesco Negri, that summed it up well:

"Here the world ends, as does my curiosity, and I shall now turn homewards, God willing … "

If only Francesco, if only. There was no prospect of going home just yet. I'd been on board the *Hurtigruten* for days, but I still had a fair distance to go to Kirkenes, as the ship swung eastwards, steering a route through deep, blue waters and edging its way between islands and snow-capped rock bluffs. It seemed impossible that anyone lived out here, but we kept stopping at fishing villages sitting amid an eerie, rock-bound landscape stripped bare by the elements. Red-painted boats bobbed in harbours overlooked by crowding crags, and seabirds wheeled and shrieked above the engine noise as we inched our way in. At every port, however small, someone would get off, something improbable would be unloaded – cases of dried fish, furniture, a bicycle – and someone else would get on.

At Vardø – Norway's most easterly town! Don't all rush off the boat at once – they seemed very proud of their one and only tree, a rowan sheltered inside the remains of an eighteenth-century, star-shaped fortress. At Vadsø, a bleary-eyed, sleep-deprived travel writer got confused – haven't I just been here? – by the lack of consonants and vowels made available by the Norwegian authorities for town-naming.

Finally, Kirkenes hove into view – population around four thousand, hard by the Russian border, four hundred kilometres north of the Arctic Circle, two thousand five hundred kilometres from Oslo, and as far east as St Petersburg and Istanbul.

On the one hand, it seemed almost churlish to turn around and leave again, given the effort involved in getting here. It was a very long ride just to say that I'd been. On the other hand, what was I getting off for? Kirkenes suffered more air raids than anywhere else in Europe except Malta during World War II; it was torched by the retreating German army who left only a dozen houses standing. When the Russians liberated the town, they found the locals hiding in the nearby iron-ore mines. It's been rebuilt since, of course, in a uniform grid stretching back from the harbour, but you could say there wasn't a lot of Kirkenes left in Kirkenes. In addition, the sun doesn't rise here between November and the end of January – at all – and even in summer there is a distinct chill. I could see my breath rising in the air. It was the middle of August.

I spent a couple of hours before the ship turned round, walking the plain streets, hands in pockets, looking for things to write about. I like to think my eventual account of the town in the *Rough Guide to Scandinavia* was useful to someone, though looking back at it now, I sense the words "grim," "end of the line" and "grit your teeth" may not have been super-helpful to the local tourist board. I also see that I suggested potential visitors might like to camp in the freezing summer climes at the local campsite, seven kilometres away – no bus, not my problem – and avoid taking photographs of any Russian military installations. This really was a specialist destination and no mistake.

Rough Guides wanted its writers to report back with a realistic, personal take on towns, regions and countries. I wasn't getting paid expenses or being put up in fancy hotels, so Scandinavia was a tougher writing gig than, say, Greece (which, I couldn't help noticing, the original founders of Rough Guides had kept for themselves). Given the sheer logistics of covering so much ground with so little money, I doubt I was very fair to many of the places I covered on that first trip ("Alta is not the kind of place anyone would want to spend much time" – "Thankfully, moving on quickly from Harstad is possible"). Apologies from the future, Alta and Harstad.

Then again, all the people I knew who used Rough Guides and Lonely Planet books didn't have any money either but still wanted to know how to get around exciting places on a budget. There was no point telling readers that Kirkenes was a "hidden gem" or a "must-see" tourist sight, when it wasn't, so I wrote what I saw, which is largely on the rather blunt lines described above. I didn't need to beguile anyone with false or unrealistic information. The journey itself was the adventure, an unforgettable boat ride around every kink of the Norwegian coast to the Russian border. Who wouldn't want to do that, whether you ended up going all the way to Kirkenes or not?

In any case, because of the challenge and the expense involved, I was fairly confident that no backpacker would ever arrive in Kirkenes clutching a copy of the *Rough Guide to Scandinavia*. As it happened, I never received a single communication about Kirkenes from readers (or, indeed, have ever met anyone else who has been there). And back in the day, I got a lot of mail about places I'd written about, sometimes in green ink, usually complaining that the price of the meal was five cents more than I'd said, or similar. Believe me, I'd have got letters about Kirkenes if anyone had ever walked to that campsite and back to discover it was closed on Tuesdays and I hadn't mentioned it.

That was never the point. I'd been hired for warts-and-all travel writing by a company that thought nowhere should be off limits. It was my job to ride the *Hurtigruten* to the end of the line, on a cruise to the edge of Europe, whether or not the destination was worth it. It was my duty to get off in a town that no one has ever described as the "Athens of the North," and potter about a bit while they unloaded canned goods and widgets. And, when the horn sounded two hours later, it was all in a day's work to return to the cruise ship that wasn't a cruise ship and make one final, fruitless search for the onboard hot tub and finger buffet, before retiring for the night in a corner with my backpack as a pillow.

A love affair in Sicily

AFTER THE RELATIVE success of my first published travel guide – some people bought it and presumably went to Scandinavia on holiday, no one died – Rough Guides offered me another destination to write about.

In what was becoming a familiar process, they quickly ascertained my suitability for the gig by asking if I'd ever been to Sicily, knew where it was, or could tell them anything about it. Apparently satisfied with the answers (no, vaguely, and not really, the Mafia?), they fronted up a couple of thousand pounds as an advance and said they'd see me in a year or so with a manuscript. A couple of weeks later I was in Sicily – found it, at the bottom of Italy! – and spent the next few months embarking on a love affair that has lasted a lifetime.

I didn't know that at the time, of course. I just thought I'd come to write a guidebook.

There wasn't another proper guidebook to Sicily at the time, which made my job a *whole* lot harder, but others had been before me, notably D.H. Lawrence. For a couple of years in the early 1920s he and his wife, Frieda, lived in a villa in the resort town of Taormina on the island's northeast coast. Lawrence was notoriously hard to please ("... perhaps the most foul-tempered writer of all time," according to Martin Amis) but even he was rather taken with Taormina, where he wrote that he had a "big, beautiful house" with a garden full of flowers overlooking the sea. The winter climate was mild and agreeable. Also, said Lawrence, his money went further in Sicily than back in England. These all seemed like very good reasons to base myself in Taormina.

There are few places in the world I've been that are so immediately captivating. The town hugs sheer crags high above the glinting Ionian Sea, with sandy bays and pebbled inlets far below stretching in either direction. The small main square and its medieval church and clocktower sit on a cliff-edge terrace with the most fabulous views. An ancient amphitheatre, cut into the hillside by its Hellenistic architects, looks across to the perfect cone of Mount Etna, rising behind the stage scenery. Narrow, stepped alleys rise off a snaking main street lined with honey-stoned palaces and mansions, with sculpted arches and gateways leading to terracotta courtyards filled with tubs of oleander and orange trees. Towers, turrets, roofs and terraces climb in tiers up the rock-bound hillside, and every sheer wall and sun-cracked façade drips with bougainvillea, wisteria, jacaranda and jasmine. It's pretty much perfect, and you can see why it warmed the cockles of even David Herbert's curmudgeonly old heart. I thought I would be able to write beautifully here, gazing out over inspiring views and breathing in the scent of the coming spring.

By the time he arrived in Sicily, Lawrence had already published *Sons and Lovers*, *The Rainbow* and *Women in Love*, and found accommodation in a villa with literary connections. I'd written the *Rough Guide to Scandinavia* – disappointingly light on destructive sexual tension, not bad on bus timetables – and hadn't bargained on Taormina being quite so flash and expensive. The best I could afford was an out-of-season holiday apartment in Giardini-Naxos, the closest beach resort, which was three kilometres away and a long way down from Taormina itself. I pointed at a picture in an estate agent's window, signed an impenetrable contract and moved in the same day.

It might have seemed that way to me at the start, but living in Giardini-Naxos was not a second-best choice. Taormina is outstandingly beautiful, but it's not the place to learn about life in Sicily.

Until I discovered there was a bus, I trudged up the very steep hill from the waterside train station – a half-hour slog to Taormina – and spent a few days wandering the flower-decked streets. No question, it was used to tourists with money and even in winter Taormina put its best face forward. Fancy boutiques and stylish restaurants lined the main Corso Umberto and if you sat down anywhere outside at a café table with starched white tablecloths, you could expect to spend a month's rent on a cappuccino. Fifteenth-century palaces advertised concerts and recitals, while in the immaculate public gardens well-dressed women in furs and gents in blazers strolled under lines of pencil-thin cypress trees. Once I'd visited the ancient theatre and climbed to the ruins of the hilltop castle, I'd seen all of Taormina and discovered next-to-nothing about living in Sicily.

In Giardini-Naxos, though, things were different. The tourist season didn't start until May, so the sweeping beach remained unswept and unkempt, empty of deckchairs, parasols and people. I could walk its whole length unimpeded, past the boarded-up lidos, picking up shells and driftwood, and then wander on my own around the scant, ancient Greek ruins of Naxos at the far end. In the other direction, I could dip my feet in rockpools by the picture-perfect islet of Isola Bella and skim stones in the calm waters.

Behind the beach, the town sprawled along the bay in a tight grid of low-rise concrete buildings and apartments, including my own, set a few blocks back from the seafront. There was a partial view if I craned my neck from one end of the balcony, but really I only went out there to hang wet clothes on the washing line and watch my socks slither off into the narrow gap between me and the next building. The apartment was barely furnished and unheated, with tile floors and thin curtains, but Sicily stayed warm throughout February and then March, and I started to fill notebooks at the dining room table.

I learned some new Italian words fairly quickly, starting with *bombola*, which I had hoped never to use. On being shown around the apartment, the agent opened a cupboard in the kitchen, pointed at a gas tank that fed the oven and hobs, explained it was the *bombola* but not to worry, it was full of gas and would never run out. Naturally, it ran out on my third day in the apartment, but not to worry, the agent had also pointed at a telephone number fixed to the cupboard. If I called that, the *bombola* man would come and all would be well.

"So all I do is call that number and ... ?"

"Yes, yes, but not to worry, it will not run out."

The only place to make a call was the local bar, which had a big, rotary-dial phone on a huge, long lead that was handed over by the barman on request. So that was now two things that I had to ask for in Italian – a telephone and a gas bottle – and I didn't really fancy my chances.

Phone in hand at one end of the bar, interested locals grouped together at the other – this was better than the telly – I made the call. I spoke a bit of Italian, but it was mostly from the *prosciutto* and *formaggio* end of the phrasebook; handy for pizza-ordering, not so great for *bombola*-wrangling.

I thought I acquitted myself reasonably well under the circumstances. In my mind, as I spoke to Signor Bombola, I could hear myself saying, "I'm terribly sorry, but would you mind awfully bringing me a new gas *bombola*, I'm the Englishman in the apartment, thank you so much, very kind of you."

Sadly, the locals at the other end of the bar almost certainly heard me barking, "Gas. Need Now. English. Come."

Amazingly, Signor Bombola did come – there was clearly only one foreigner in a chilly apartment in out-of-season Giardini-Naxos that year. He put-putted up on a Vespa with a rear flat-back, hoisted the *bombola* over his shoulder, climbed several flights of stairs to my apartment and then switched gas tanks, all the time offering an indecipherable running commentary – presumably along the lines of, "Yes, my mates in the bar said there was a foreigner in town, from Milan are you? Thought so, terrible accent, anyway that's a million *lire*, plus the extra, you know, for being from Milan."

All the time, incidentally, his Vespa was running on idle outside the building, sounding like a shotgun going off at intervals, which was another thing about Giardini – and therefore Sicily – that I was slowly coming to terms with.

It was incessantly and insanely loud, from morning until night. Not up in lovely Taormina it wasn't, where church bells broke the overnight silence and white-gloved waiters swept crumbs off table linen with little hand-held sweepers. But down in Sicily, in Giardini, the racket started at dawn with the street cleaners – municipal slogan: No bin goes un-banged – and ended in the small hours when the café owners pulled down their metal rollers with the admirable enthusiasm of toddlers in a tin-can factory.

Traffic shot up and down every street, engines gunning, horns blaring, squealing to a halt at junctions and traffic lights – not, by the way, through any sense of safety or adherence to the Highway Code but just to shout through open windows at friends, colleagues, enemies and strangers. In Sicily it's basically a lottery if the cars move again when the traffic lights turn green; it depends on whether you've finished your chat or not.

Parking was also considered optional, or at least parking as you might know it. Instead of manoeuvring into orderly lines by the kerbside, cars simply screeched to a stop at a convenient place for the driver – straddling traffic lanes, half on the pavement, wheels in the shop doorway, you name it. What often looked like a tangled, multi-vehicle pile-up usually just turned out to be people waiting for the butcher to open. If someone came out of a shop to find their car boxed in – a hundred-percent possibility on any given day in Giardini – the recognised method of extracting their vehicle from the melee was first to start the engine and give the surrounding cars a bit of a nudge and, if that didn't shift them sufficiently, go to work on the horn. After about five minutes of vigorous tooting – with cars from several streets away joining in out of sympathy – the transgressing owner would usually emerge from a shop, shouting loudly, and then move the vehicle just enough to let one car out and block another in, all the while adding to the uproar by having a go on his own horn.

It was bedlam. People seemed to yell at each other for no apparent reason – unnerving if all you're trying to do is buy an orange – but as these apparent confrontations never turned into fist fights I eventually figured that life was just switched up to ten here, in a way that it never was in England.

I swiftly discovered another new word, thanks to the man who trundled his cart up and down outside my apartment most days, shouting his head off about *carciofi*. (And by "shouting his head off," I mean "expressing himself at an entirely normal volume for a Sicilian.") Artichokes, it turned out – and I felt that word was going to prove a whole lot more useful than *bombola* because I could use it in a restaurant.

While Giardini was a resort, it was also a working town, so the cafés and restaurants stayed open during winter. I ate in a family-run place down the road a few times a week – Fratelli Marano, the "Marano Brothers," it's still there – and slowly ordered my way through a menu that bore little resemblance to those at home. Mussels in a spicy tomato broth, deep-fried courgette flowers stuffed with ricotta, spaghetti with fresh tuna and peas, pasta with fried aubergine and salted cheese – this wasn't the Italian food I knew, and it turned out that it wasn't Italian food at all, at least as far as the waiters were concerned. It was Sicilian and don't you forget it, an attitude epitomised by the after-dinner drink that came whether you wanted it or not. Sure, you could have a *grappa* or a brandy, but first you were going to get a shot of *amaro Averna*, a strange liqueur (*amaro* means bitter) from the hill town of Caltanissetta. Reputedly invented by a pharmacist, it's a bracing, supercharged, alcoholic concoction of herbs and roots that's half cold-remedy, half hair-of-the-dog reviver. Once past the interesting smell it's down in one and hold on tight, and then who knows what the night may bring?

Food and food-shopping – those were the two ways into Sicily and its culture as far as I was concerned. I was officially – just about – a travel writer with a published book to my name, but as that book was about Scandinavia I'd previously found it difficult to embrace the cuisine. Take the typical Swedish dish of *surströmming*, which is basically herring that you bury in the ground for six months until it rots and then dig up and eat. In Sicily, though, every new day brought a taste revelation, from breakfast onwards, which if you wanted, could be a split brioche stuffed with ice cream accompanied by a shot of brandy in your espresso. At least, that's what the policeman who called into my local bar had most days.

The only shops in Giardini were the sort of proper shops that were dying out in England – fishmonger, greengrocer, butcher, baker and, I dare say, candlestick-maker. To put together a meal, you had to spend half a day walking around town, visiting several stores, rather than driving to an out-of-town supermarket in a four-wheel drive Subaru. No wonder nothing else ever got done – you could easily spend another full day in the local post office trying to buy a stamp from the one open counter because the rest of the staff were out shopping.

The produce available was extraordinary, even the things that I recognised, such as tomatoes and lemons. These were like no tomatoes or lemons that had ever been sold at home in Yorkshire, that's for sure – piled high and not plastic-wrapped, and of hugely varying size, colour and shape. Not only did they look and taste different – more intense and flavourful, more tomatoey and lemony – but there were different varieties for different uses and dishes, which was news to Yorkshire where a small, round, hard, flavourless "salad tomato" did duty for every conceivable occasion. The little Pachino cherry tomatoes from Sicily's southeast were tiny flavour bombs, to be slugged in olive oil and sprinkled with the dried, wild oregano that was sold in hanging bunches. For salads, you'd slice thin rounds from enormous knobbly tomatoes that veered from green to white to red on the same specimen; and for pasta sauce, there were the elongated plum tomatoes on musky stalks that, until that point, I had only ever encountered preserved in a tin.

The greengrocer in Giardini was where I solved the mystery of the *carciofi* and other hitherto-unknown foodstuffs – fennel (*finocchio*), chicory (*radicchio*), medlars (*nespole*), quince (*mela cotogna*), rocket (*rucola*), figs (*fichi*), pine nuts (*pinoli*), even the prickly pear (*fichi d'India*) that grew wild up the steps into Taormina. The fishmonger had trays of fresh, raw prawns in different sizes, as well as whole squid, slabs of tuna and mounds of pink-sheened red mullet, which was so cheap they virtually gave it away. Even on a travel writer's limited budget, I could afford to fry up a handful of prawns with fat slices of garlic and follow it with a whole grilled fish for dinner. The butcher sold vivid rings of Mortadella or sliced salami that I learned to order an *etto* (a hundred grammes) at a time. On Sunday mornings at the bakery you could buy fresh pasta in intriguing shapes with names to savour – *busiate, anelletti, spaccatelle* – and on Sunday evenings, when you couldn't be bothered to cook, you could nip down to the spit-roast chicken shop for a takeaway *pollo arrosto* which leaked spicy grease through the waxed paper.

In restaurants I started marrying up my rapidly expanding vocabulary with menu choices that didn't sound as if they could possibly be right but turned out to be delicious. Peeled and sliced orange in a vinaigrette dressing; spaghetti with anchovies and dried breadcrumbs; pasta with sardines and wild fennel; swordfish steaks rolled around raisins, pine nuts and capers? All *bona fide* Sicilian dishes and not the result of the chef having a breakdown or an error in translation.

Winter started to turn into spring in early February, which came as another surprise. Wildflowers and scented herbs carpeted the hillsides behind Taormina and the almond blossom flowered exuberantly. The days turned noticeably warmer and – unable to believe that you could sit outside and eat in March – I turned to T-shirts and then shorts, though I was in a distinct minority of one. No Sicilian removes their winter coat or scarf until the temperature hits twenty degrees Celsius and, even then, it's touch and go some days. I suspect there's an agreed date only vouchsafed to locals, possibly transmitted by text message, because on one day everyone's dressed like the winds are whistling in from the Kazakh steppe and the next they're all in designer Ts and Armani sunglasses.

Using Giardini as a base, I saw more of the island, travelling by bus and train and filling yet more notebooks. I was a boy from the Cold North and here in Europe's Deep South I found my place in the sun.

If at the start I thought that I had come to write about Italy, I was dead wrong. Sicily was – is – gloriously, fundamentally different. Ancient Greek temples line the ridge below the town of Agrigento; dazzling Byzantine mosaics adorn towering medieval churches; while white cube houses and minarets dot towns with Arabic roots where couscous is served in the local restaurants. Baroque-styled cities on an epic scale make a film-set of the southeast; a commuter train circumnavigates Europe's most active volcano, Mount Etna; and craggy offshore islands of even more mystery and allure hang off the Sicilian coast like pendants. The entire human record of the Mediterranean is

44

here, from Phoenician to Greek, Arab to Norman, Spanish to Italian, crammed onto a wild, mountainous island in a sparkling sea.

I fell in love with it all, soaking up a culture and life that six months earlier I didn't really know existed. Partly, I'm sure, it was the juxtaposition. I'd just spent the best part of two years travelling around and then writing about Scandinavia, where the sun never got out in winter and pizzas were topped with tinned pineapple and salt-cod, a combo I've still never seen anywhere else. In Sicily, I was lounging by harbours in bare feet in April and discovering that there were only three things, four at the most, that were ever permissible on a pizza.

"But why can't I have mushrooms *and* anchovies on my pizza?"

"Because they don't go together." An entirely normal response by a Sicilian waiter.

But mostly I loved it because this was a place, a landscape and a cuisine that spoke to me.

I awoke most days to a warm sun and piercing blue skies. I caught the bus to distant hill villages and walked through heady citrus groves to isolated medieval monasteries. In the distance, on the skyline, Etna puffed and panted. Ancient ruins – Roman, Greek and even older – lay abandoned in rock-bound valleys, and I scuffed my way through wild marigolds and marjoram to find hand-cut stones and toppled buildings that skittered with crickets and lizards.

The people were kind and generous – once they'd established that I was properly foreign and not just Italian – and

I was invited into homes for meals. Also out to restaurants for meals. Encouraged to try things in shops and on trains. Given samples of things in bars. Basically, fed at every opportunity by people who knew that this was the best food on the planet; who had taken it to New York and Melbourne and said, there you go, no, not Italian, Sicilian.

In the capital Palermo's *souk*-like markets – possibly the closest you can get to time travel, where medieval life simply carries on and damn the modern world – I wandered through alleys lined with pigs' heads, barrels of olives and mounds of saffron. Hardware salesmen banged tin buckets to get my attention and I was pressured into trying *pane ca meusa* from a metal cauldron – a fried spleen sandwich in a sesame roll, one of those things about which you later say, "Well it wasn't the *worst* thing I've ever eaten."

Down the coast from Taormina in the second city of Catania, the huge outdoor market spreads across another confusing warren of streets. In the fish market, the *Pescheria*, burly men with wickedly sharp knives carved huge steaks off sides of tuna that were more than a metre long. Swordfish heads – sword intact, pointing up to the sky – stood on trestle tables, and for a mid-morning snack you could join the line for a beer and a raw, cut-open, sea urchin, a *riccio di mare*, doused with lemon.

As the months went by, I came down more regularly to Catania and the market, thinking that in many ways this was the distillation of all that I loved about Sicily. The noise, the life, the colour – yes, all those vague characterisations loved by travel writers were certainly there in abundance.

But it was more than that. It was the slow realisation that life didn't have to be like it was at home. It could be like this, every day. England was as much on the edge of Europe as Sicily, but imagine plonking a swordfish head on a table at the local market there, or serving up a fried-entrail sandwich with tongs from a bucket. There are laws about that sort of thing; what would the Parish Council say; and could you please stop shouting about your artichokes. The more I saw of Sicily, the more I thought that I probably belonged somewhere else other than England.

There was a little trattoria at the back of the *Pescheria* and, if it's not still there thirty years later, there will be another just like it somewhere nearby. There was no menu, because the owner just cooked whatever she bought from the market that day, which raged on outside as early morning turned towards noon and thoughts of lunch. You sat down where you could and, for about six quid all-in, you got a half-litre of local wine – rough as a rat-catcher's glove, fine after the first glass – and three courses produced from a barebones stove in her open kitchen.

There was always pasta, of course, followed by a choice of *pesce* or *carne*, fish or meat, which was the only clue you got. Could be swordfish or chicken, could be squid or ox tongue, it didn't do to be fussy. Having made your selection, the owner got to work on the grill, all the while mincing garlic and parsley and putting together a simple salad. At some point – not every visit, but enough times to make it entirely normal – she'd realise she was out of some key ingredient, which didn't put the slightest stop to her gallop. She'd simply raise a window and bellow out into the market, in the manner of a buffalo farmer calling home the herd, and keep on bellowing – over the shouting, the revving Vespas, the delivery truck engines and a thousand loudly gesticulating Sicilians – until a harassed stallholder delivered what was required, accompanied by even more shouting on both sides.

No one in the restaurant, of course, raised so much as an eyebrow. They just got on with eating lunch and wincing at the wine, in the middle of the organised tumult that was not just the *Pescheria* but Sicily.

I wrote it all down, every word, and fell completely and hopelessly in love.

A comfort break in China

IT'S FIVE HUNDRED kilometres from the southeastern city of Guangzhou to the dramatic karst mountains of Guilin. On a decent road, in a decent bus, the journey is scheduled to take eight to ten hours, though no one in the ticket office is prepared to put an actual figure on it.

But a few hours out of Guangzhou – still a long way from Guilin – the roads are anything but decent. And the bus could be kindly described as a piece of crap. Actually, several pieces of crap spot-welded together, with torn seats, challenging suspension and thin cotton blinds that billow out of permanently open window vents. It's a hot and bumpy ride, and orange dust swirls up from the dry verges and settles on seatbacks, window frames and any upper arm that's braced against the jolts.

So it's basically your average Chinese bus, which stops every now and again to cram on an ever more improbable number of passengers, carrying their ever more improbable pieces of luggage. Bags and boxes are not the half of it, though they take up every overhead space and most of the aisle. There are

49

baskets and wrapped packages that move and make snuffling sounds – puppies or kittens is the best and most hopeful guess – and long, canvas-wrapped items that could be fishing rods, scaffolding poles, lances, stilts or puppy-pacifiers, who knows. There's market shopping, containers of goods and tools, rolls of cloth and bundles of fabric and clothes. You could joke about there being everything but the kitchen sink on here, except someone almost certainly has packed a ceramic basin or two. It's less a bus, more a bazaar on wheels.

No one ever seems to get off, so over the hours the vehicle has gradually filled to capacity and then some, with whole families seemingly squeezed into two adjacent seats. Most of the front and back is jammed full and the only part of the bus where there is any semblance of space are the middle two rows. Where we are. The backpackers: the only ones who got on at the beginning of the journey and won't be getting off until the very end; the only ones not making the trip for family, business or commercial reasons.

There's even a spare seat among us, which has a backpack on it but which at every stop is manoeuvred between someone's legs so that a new or existing passenger could sit down properly. Without exception, they all take a look at the seat, take a look at the foreigners – still a relative rarity – decide against it and proceed to wedge themselves in further back between a bale of cotton T-shirts and a two-grandma family perched on the wheel arch.

Aside from picking up passengers, there has been one leg-stretch stop and, more recently, one unexplained halt by the side of the road. We sit there with the engine idling, doors closed, while the driver pushes buttons and pulls levers on his dashboard. Whatever is supposed to happen apparently doesn't, because he slaps the steering wheel in frustration and shouts imprecations. When the bus starts again it shudders and groans like a pensioner getting up from an armchair, before settling into a lurching half-pace down a highway riddled with potholes. We bounce and bang a bit further, which sets off alarmed yelping from the boxed puppies up back, until finally the bus pulls into a roadside clearing by a wooden shack. The driver switches the engine off, and the powering-down sounds like the life support being pulled. He announces something unintelligible to us, but which goes down badly with the rest of the passengers, who all tumble out of the front door while muttering furiously.

Best guess, broken-down bus. A guess supported by the sight of the driver taking metal tools out of a canvas bag and raising the bonnet with a resigned look in his eye.

We are last out of the bus, which means we are last in line for the toilets and the makeshift café inside the shack. We stand around for a bit, a mixed group of nationalities, uncertain what to do or how long we'll have to do it for. The ferocious clanking from under the bonnet, punctuated by the deep sighs of a driver who knows he's not getting paid overtime, suggests that we could be here for a while. We have no idea where "here" is; Guilin still seems an awful long way away.

Someone volunteers to go around the corner and investigate the toilet facilities, and comes back ashen-faced.

"If you're a bloke and it's a number one, I'd just join those guys," and he gestures at the line of men standing twenty metres away, backs to the road, watering the dust.

"But if you need to squat or it's a number two … well it doesn't look good. I'd hold on if you can."

His subsequent description, while eloquent, makes no sense to Westerners with a keen sense of what a toilet should look like. In the end, we all have to go and see for ourselves.

Behind the shack are a couple of small brick houses with laundry on lines and chickens scratching in the dirt. Between the houses and the shack is a series of waist-high pens or stalls set on a rough concrete floor. There are metal pans inside each stall, and each pan and stall is connected to a section of sloping, open guttering which moves the contents – numbers one and two – down to a sort of holding cell. There's a water bowl and a pile of rags by each stall, and shovels and buckets nearby. There are also pigs in an adjacent pen, which seem inordinately excited by the spattering sounds and exotic aromas.

Our fellow backpacker is correct. This does not look good. This does not look like a facility anyone would be keen to use. Even so, we recognise some of the other passengers taking full advantage of this unexpected comfort break, and we recognise them because – even employing an acrobatic low squat – the stall walls are at just the right height to be on nodding terms with your neighbour. Turn your head right or left while otherwise employed and you could have a nice chat, as indeed some friends and family are doing.

We all resolve to hold on if we can.

Inside the shack, a few plastic tables and chairs are laid out as a rudimentary café. It's clearly set up for passing trade and a few of the passengers are already eating from rice bowls. The kitchen appears to be a counter with a couple of gas rings, some outsized cooking pots and a shelf lined with soft drinks. There's no menu and the person behind the counter – having established that we're all foreigners – makes a concerted effort not to catch anyone's eye or offer any assistance.

We're mostly used to this by now. It's not really prejudice or rudeness; rather, it's a question of not losing face. In the bigger cities, where tourism is growing and students learn English, you can expect to be approached and engaged in conversation in parks, cafés and restaurants. I'd had my hair cut in a barber's shop in Guangzhou and – highly visible in the window – the twenty-minute operation turned into two hours as a procession of students came in to try out their English. At some point someone brought in tea and I had to sit there, hair half-cut, discussing the weather in England, the optimal number of brothers and sisters in a family, and Manchester United. But out in the sticks it's much less common to see foreigners, and people avoid interaction because they fear embarrassing both themselves and these guests in their country. They don't speak English and don't know how to deal with us and our weird ways and demands. It's why no one will sit next to us on the bus – the potential for public humiliation is just too great. And it's why you can sit at a café table in a roadside shack and have the owner pretend you're not there.

Eventually, we copy what the other passengers are doing, which is to stand at the counter, look into the couple of open pots and point. Someone has a phrasebook and a few words of Chinese, which results in bowls of rice, some stir-fried tofu and a dish of mixed vegetables all round. More pointing brings a tray of lukewarm drinks from the shelf.

Emboldened by this relative success – and with no sign of the bus being ready to move – the person with the phrasebook thinks more food is in order.

"Chicken? What do you say we order some chicken between us?"

There's a to and fro at the counter, as our backpacker friend points at the word and says something that they hope approximates to "chicken", and the café owner repeats something that sounds vaguely similar several times with a rising, querying intonation. There's much nodding on both sides as the deal appears to be sealed. Our travelling companion comes back to the table, flushed with success, and the owner disappears behind a curtain at the back of the kitchen area.

There's silence for a minute or two, while we pass round the rice and vegetables and start our meal. There's some desultory conversation about where we might be and how far we are from Guilin.

A few more minutes pass before there's a shout from somewhere out the back, behind the curtain, and then a furious, indignant squawking. We look at each other as other sounds ring out loudly – frantic scuffles, further shouting, more and louder squawking, and then a sudden and very final thud.

"You don't think, do you … ?"

We examine the evidence. Everyone who's eaten anything here so far has eaten from the two pots we can see on the counter. The drinks aren't refrigerated. There doesn't seem to be any electric power at all. It's too hot to keep pre-prepared raw food on hand.

Yes, we do think.

Over the next thirty minutes the sounds continue behind the curtain – first some grunting, and then assorted shuffling and scraping noises, followed by the pouring and draining of water, and finally a flurry of what sounds suspiciously like cleaver chops on wood. Our initial meal is long finished, the bowls and chopsticks pushed into the centre of the table. All the other diners have left too and are standing outside the shack watching the driver still wrestling with the innards of the bus.

The café owner materialises from behind his curtain with a heaped plate, heats a giant wok on the gas and throws in ingredients from under the counter. He's sweating profusely – indeed, like someone who has just gone three rounds in the summer heat with a feisty chicken – and wields a clattering metal spatula the size of a spade. Another five minutes and he slides the stir-fried contents of the wok onto a large plastic platter and delivers it to the table, with more rice and new bowls. He smiles, grimly we feel, and retires safely behind the counter, clearly hoping not to have anything more to do with foreigners today.

The chicken has been prepared in the Chinese way; that is to say, chopped into bite-sized pieces across the bone. On the plus side, parts of it are definitely cooked but, then again, other parts definitely aren't. Some of the bones and joints sit in raw flesh and there are flecks of blood on the platter. The very yellow and wrinkly chicken skin is mostly intact too, and there are feather stubs and tufts on some of the pieces. Even if this was the world's tastiest-looking chicken, rather than the interrupted medical experiment currently on display, it is still the case that we have all seen where that chicken once lived, pecking around the toilet facilities out back.

A few make a valiant effort to at least try the dish, though noticeably not the instigator, who appears to be distancing themself from the entire affair by muttering that that's not what they ordered. Like the mistake is one of translation and not of an entire social and cultural misunderstanding. The only person to come out of this with any credit is the café owner, who – asked, for some unaccountable reason, by unfathomable foreigners, for something that wasn't on the menu – went out and grabbed a chicken, as requested, and dished it up in double-quick time so that the foreigners, guests in his country, wouldn't miss their bus which, oh look, now appears to be spluttering into life again.

There's a yell from the bus driver, who then has to stand back as his passengers pour on board, clambering over bags, boxes and luggage to reclaim their seats. They leave the middle rows alone, considerately, and watch out of the windows as we peel off a thick wedge of *yuan* notes to pay for the meal – in reality, a dollar or so a head, chicken and cabaret plus toilet facilities included.

Last off when it broke down, we're also last back on the bus, shuffling up the aisle past a now largely indifferent crowd who just want to reach Guilin before nightfall. As we leave the shack, the café owner – nothing if not thoughtful – presses the remainder of the chicken dish on us, decanted into a plastic bag. He obviously doesn't have high hopes for us getting to our destination before the next mealtime.

As we retake our seats, the bag gets passed from one to another until it ends up – rightly, by general agreement – with the person who thought that ordering roadhouse chicken would be a good idea. The only place for the bag of gently oozing, semi-cooked, meat to go is on their lap, which is where it remains as we bounce slowly down the dust-filled road in the dusk towards Guilin.

A night on the tiles in Portugal

IN OUR DEFENCE, we're English. Where we come from, drinks are bought and paid for at the bar, in advance of the actual drinking. It's a sensible system and everyone knows where they stand. Pay first, drink second. Pay again. Drink more.

Also in our defence, we are engaged in a heated debate about the films *Mad Max* and *Mad Max 2*.

Obviously, there's no question about the relative merits of the films, *Mad Max 2* clearly being the finer, more accomplished work – as with *The Godfather: Part II* or *Aliens*, so with Mel Gibson's second go at the whole drifter-cop-apocalypse scenario. No, the real argument is quite how mad Max is in the first film, the prevailing opinion being that it might have been better titled *Slightly Cross Max*. Whereas by *Mad Max 2* he is definitely at the more furious end of the scale, though still not irrefutably crazy. And as we are killing time at a pavement bar in Lisbon before a matinée showing of *Mad Max: Beyond Thunderdome*, we're naturally keen to establish the parameters of Max-madness before seeing the movie for the first time.

So there's already been some drinking – outdoors in the sun, to make things worse – and minds have been occupied in serious debate. A dickie-bowed waiter has been delivering trays of ice-cold Super Bock beers to our pavement table and doing a fine job of it, can't complain at all, when someone notices the time. Five minutes until the start of the film. As one, we're up out of our seats and legging it unsteadily down Avenida da Liberdade towards the cinema, when someone says:

"Just a thought. We forgot to pay."

As I say, not entirely our fault, what with being English and distracted and everything.

We pause outside the cinema. Admittedly, it's not a good look – three red-faced English visitors doing a runner from a bar. It's embarrassing because we're not those kinds of visitors, heavens no. Between us, we've got more masters degrees (two) than tattoos (zero) and, let's face it, our idea of a lads' holiday is a city break to the gentle and cultured capital of Portugal.

That said, no one wants to miss *Mad Max: Beyond Thunderdome*. It's been several years since *Mad Max 2* came out; Mel must be positively barking by now. Also, and unsaid but silently acknowledged, no one wants to go back and face an irate Portuguese waiter.

Two hours later, after the film, we all realise the error of our ways. *Beyond Thunderdome* is terrible – *Godfather 3*, *Alien Resurrection* terrible. If you've never seen it, two words: Tina Turner. Fine singer, ruthless post-apocalyptic ruler, not so much.

There's a short discussion about the etiquette of returning to the avenue bar and explaining why it's taken several hours to realise our mistake. We're definitely going to do that, no question, we're responsible tourists, but it might be a bit awkward and no one knows the Portuguese for "We're the ones who ran away. Yes, to see *Beyond Thunderdome*. We know, terrible. How much do we owe you?"

Absolutely, we're going to do that. Rude not to. But first, more drinks.

"Bairro Alto?" We're all agreed.

Lisbon's neighbourhoods – its *bairros* – are strung across the plains and slopes of several hills that stretch back from the river, the Rio Tejo. There's the castle and the Alfama neighbourhood on one side, the flat, lower town – known as the Baixa – in the middle and, on the punishingly steep hill above us, the upper town, the Bairro Alto. Personally, I'd put my bars on the lower, flat bit – make it all a bit easier to stagger from one to another without slipping on the cobbles. Each to their own though. Lisbon's main bar scene is high up in the Bairro Alto, an undulating grid of narrow streets laid out in the sixteenth century and lined with tall, shuttered, tiled townhouses.

Back in the 1980s, when I first started spending a lot of time in Portugal for Rough Guides, Lisbon was different from other European capitals – not the hipster destination it is now, but faded, elegant and fun, if a bit rough around the edges. However, even then – as now – the Bairro Alto was the place for a good night out. Those townhouses hid a rare selection of bars and clubs behind barn-like wooden doors and small windows with iron grilles. Half of them didn't even have names – they either threw open the doors to the street and served beers from a makeshift bar at the back of what was once a warehouse, or you had to ring a bell and hope you looked the part. As the Bairro Alto was also historically the Red Light zone, ringing the wrong bell was always a distinct possibility – let's just say it added a *frisson* to the whole experience.

Up we go to the Bairro Alto, jumping on the Ascensor da Glória, the antique funicular railway that connects lower and upper towns. The street it clanks up is so horrendously steep that the ascending carriage is raised at one end so that you sit or stand on a level surface and don't just tumble down in a heap at the back. It's also rather stately and slow, which is fine if you're enjoying a sightseeing ride up to one of Lisbon's most characteristic neighbourhoods; not so handy, for example, if you're using it as a getaway vehicle after a bar runner.

The *ascensor* is not even the most joyfully ridiculous form of public transport from the Baixa up to the Bairro Alto. That would be the Elevador de Santa Justa, a stunning wrought-iron lift with wood-panelled carriages that whisks you up fifty metres and seven storeys in a matter of minutes. It's as if someone has removed the elevator from a hotel in a Wes Anderson film and just left it there on the street. When people ask why I love Lisbon, these elegant, archaic survivors, that should have no place in a modern city, are a huge part of the reason.

The *ascensor* drops us at the top of the hill, by shady gardens with a sprawling view over downtown Lisbon. Right across the street is a bar with no name that we have fallen into and out of several times on previous visits, and it's now a traditional stop for a first or last drink in the *bairro*. It has a stainless-steel door, metal bars on the windows and a chipped formica counter-top inside, behind which stands the burly proprietor. There's a half-hearted football pennant on the wall behind him and a clock that doesn't tell the time. Otherwise, the only indication that it is actually a bar is the enormous chest-fridge, into which the owner reaches for cans of Sagres beer the minute anyone walks through the door. There's no point asking for anything else.

The bar is known to us all as the "Rufty-Tufty Bar" on account of the occasion it got a bit rough, tough and rowdy late one night as we were waiting for the funicular. Somebody said something untoward, voices were raised and a glass was broken, and we were about to sidle out and avoid the unpleasantness when peace was restored by the simple expedient of the proprietor producing a baseball bat and tapping it on the bar a few times, just to get everyone's attention. We felt fairly safe thereafter, even in the dodgiest bars in Lisbon, of which there were still many despite the creeping gentrification in places such as the Bairro Alto. Down by the river, behind Cais do Sodré station, for example, there was a run of garish, neon-lit music bars on Rua dos Remolares where employing the phrase "Hello sailor" could either get you a good time, no questions asked, or a good kicking by actual sailors. It was hit and miss, to be honest, so you had to be in the mood for either.

The "Rufty-Tufty" serves its first-drink purpose – let's not quibble about the pre-cinema beers – but it's not the place to sit awhile and browse the phrasebook's sections on 'Apologies', 'Non-payment' and 'Cultural misunderstandings'. Luckily, there's a bar virtually next door which is exactly the type of establishment that encourages lingering in deep armchairs over drinks that don't come in tins lifted from the bowels of industrial catering units.

The Port Wine Institute is more than just a bar. Once found – courtesy, the first time, of the trusty *Rough Guide* – never forgotten or passed by. The Lisbon outpost of the regulatory body of Portugal's most famous drink, the Institute occupies a grand old building of offices and meeting rooms. But tucked inside, through etched-glass doors and along gloomy corridors, is the wood-panelled tasting lounge, where you can sample pretty much any port you like at astonishingly good-value prices. It's not quite as grand as it sounds or as it likes to make out. If tramps had a gentlemen's club, it would be like Lisbon's Port Wine Institute, where suited-and-booted – but unshaven and frayed-at-the-edge – waiters hover in the background, ignoring any attempt to catch their eye. We settle into slightly stained armchairs set around smeared-glass tables and examine a leather-bound menu containing a baffling range of port wines – Ruby, Tawny, Vintage, Late Bottled Vintage, Reserve, White, Garrafeira, Colheita and Crusted. We are familiar with its well-thumbed pages. We've spent many happy hours here on past visits to Lisbon, pointing at random and saying "Go on then, that one."

If, like us, you are urbane sophisticates on a cultural tour of Neoclassical Lisbon, there is only one pre-dinner choice, which is a cheeky glass of young, bracingly crisp, white port. It does the job that sherry does, with less of the elderly aunt connotations. It's the ideal aperitif – or would be, if we hadn't already had several lunchtime Super Bocks and an emergency can of Sagres. This rather clouds our judgement, which explains why we find ourselves instead channelling Richard E. Grant and demanding "the finest wines known to humanity" from a baffled Portuguese waiter who, inexplicably, has never seen *Withnail and I*.

I'll say this for vintage port. You certainly know when you've had a bottle of heavy, red, highly alcoholic, fortified wine, especially on an empty stomach on a warm evening. Is it a wise choice? Would a doctor recommend it? On the whole, I think we'd have to say not, but the damage is done and the prospect of ending up by accident in a sailors' bar later on is rather more advanced than it was.

Fortunately, Portuguese food is designed for those occasions when you've accidentally over-drunk – or, in terms a scientist might use, when you've exposed yourself to too much yin, or possibly yang. Balance is all. If you've over-yinned – and it's easily done – then you require immediate feeding in a Portuguese restaurant. A typical meal provides three types of carbohydrate on the same plate – bread, rice and potatoes – and laughs at the concept of portion-control. It's food for the sort of people who rounded the Cape in galleons, built forts in Asia and mined gold in Brazil. You can't do that on tofu and lettuce leaves, and pity the ship's captain that suggested to burly able seamen that you could.

We revive ourselves with giant servings of roast pork and salt cod in the Bota Alta tavern, which is typical of the neighbourhood – a cramped, wood-panelled and *azulejo*-tiled diner where wine of indeterminate colour and strength comes in ceramic jugs. The food arrives on vast, stainless-steel platters that have to be carried by multiple waiters and, if you so much as clear a corner space of food, new mounds of chips and rice magically appear. These days, Bairro Alto restaurants know their way around foams, reductions and Michelin stars, but the Bota Alta – and many others of the same style and vintage – is still going strong, and would be my recommendation if you ever find yourself in Lisbon on the wrong side of a bottle of vintage port.

Down-time in the Bota Alta tavern has led to a certain amount of reflection, as we're still feeling guilty about the earlier runner. By now though, bars in the Baixa – the downtown business area – are shutting up for the night and our fleeced waiter is probably long gone. Meanwhile, outside in the Bairro Alto, things are just beginning to pick up pace. More drinks is the general consensus – obviously, first thing tomorrow, go back and pay, without question etc – especially as a quick glance at the street outside indicates that we are no longer the drunkest people in the neighbourhood. Not by a long way.

By ten pm we are being carried along in a general, good-natured horde that moves us down the narrow streets and deposits us in front of unmarked bars crowded with people drinking ice-cold beers. None of them appear to be brothels, so we fight our way in, drink a tiny beer known as an "Imperial" in each one and then join the flow again outside. Lisbon nightlife is still very much like this – fads and fashions change, and the bars are a bit more sophisticated, but a night out in the Bairro

Alto is generally a case of chucking yourself into a rolling tide of humanity and seeing where the waves dump you.

Eventually, they dump us where they always dump us at the end of an evening, outside the best bar that we know for a late-night, go-on-then, just-one-more drink before we attempt to remember where exactly it is that we are staying.

The Pavilhão Chinês – the "Chinese Pavilion" – was once a tea- and coffee-merchant's establishment and occupies another of those sober townhouses that hide so many hangovers in the Bairro Alto. Inside is a warren of rooms, each lined with glass- and mirror-fronted cabinets that contain a bizarre selection of what I'm sure someone thinks of as treasured artefacts – old plates, toy trains, medals, helmets, dolls, carvings, maps, mugs, lead soldiers, mini-battleships, statues, busts and figurines. There are whole squadrons of model aeroplanes hanging from the ceilings, not to mention any number of bells and clocks, as well as a full-size Beefeater.

When we first discovered it, we thought it was a bit of fun – it's certainly different, like someone ransacked a mad professor's house or robbed a provincial museum. To be honest, after a lot of drinks, it's a bit freaky – with so many toys, statues and dolls, it's surely only a numbers game. You'd imagine that one of them has to come alive and run amok at some point, grabbing one of the many military daggers handily displayed.

But what the Chinese Pavilion does have is a pool table and some nice, cosy booths, where young gentlemen might while away a final hour before staggering back down the road to the arms of the "Rufty Tufty", where an absolute, definite, no-really last drink awaits.

I'd like to say that this was a night to remember, though clearly it has taken many hours of hypnotherapy – and a few Proustian Super Bocks – to put together the chain of events. You'll notice, for example, that I gloss over the names of any bars encountered between the restaurant and the Pavilhão Chinês. In truth, many nights in Lisbon followed a similar pattern over the years. Sure, the details changed slightly from time to time. Like the occasion we eschewed the Bota Alta tavern in favour of an extravagantly tiled restaurant where things appeared to be going swimmingly – three types of carbs, a steady supply of jugs of wine – when the chef appeared out of the kitchen and started singing at full tilt, to be joined by the waiters, the owner and the bar staff. It turned out it was a *fado* restaurant – *fado* being a Portuguese musical genre of great melancholy and startling volume that you do not want in your earhole while eating chips. Or the time when an elderly gentleman in an ill-fitting suit showed us his gun, which – over-yinned as we were – seemed an entirely fine state of affairs rather than a cause for concern.

All these reasons I add to my list, when people ask me why I love Lisbon so much: the ludicrous public transport, the fortified wine liveners, the idiosyncratic watering holes, the Desperate-Dan-sized dinners, the exotically named beers, the Chucky doll-filled drinking emporiums, and the hill-top warren of bars where absolutely no one knows your name.

And no, we never went back and paid the bill.

A murderer on the loose in America

IT WAS ALL in the intonation.

"May God help you!" – the rising word "God" stretched out across several syllables and the "help you" a dismissive, downbeat "help ya," as the officer waved us through.

We looked at each other, put the car in drive and moved off through the roadblock, past a cordon of armed police in flak jackets.

"Is it just me, or did he really not want us to do this?"

"Oh, I think he was pretty clear on the subject."

"Did you see his gun?"

"I saw the gun."

"But we're still going, right?"

"What else are we going to do? We've got rooms booked. It's the Fourth of July weekend coming up. There's nowhere else to stay."

"There is that. There is also the fact that a heavily armed police officer just advised us definitely not to do the thing that we're just about to do".

We looked at each other, shrugged, and drove off down the road towards the Grand Canyon.

Because here's the thing about being British in America. It all seems so unreal in any case, from the first minute you arrive. It's at once so familiar and yet so alien – the classic example of two countries separated by a common language. It's not just the pavement/sidewalk, autumn/fall thing, it's the whole nine yards, to coin a phrase that makes exactly no sense if you're British. First-time reactions to America are a true blend of "Oh!", "Really?" and "What?!", as you encounter familiar things and famous places from TV and the movies – the Empire State! A yellow school bus! A neon motel sign! – alongside inexplicable puzzles like marshmallows and Jell-O on the salad bar. Jelly, I mean jelly. In cubes, in a little tray next to the Iceberg lettuce and tomato slices, like that's a regular thing to have with salad.

So when an Arizona state trooper holding a rifle tells you there's an escaped murderer on the loose in the Grand Canyon, on the one hand you go "No way! That's insane!" and, on the other, you say "Ooh it's just like those TV shows" and don't take it seriously.

We don't really have murderous escapees in England, and even if we did come across one and got ourselves kidnapped, we'd be terribly apologetic about it all and probably offer to drive the escape vehicle. We do have national parks and fascinating geological features but the worst thing that happens in those places is that someone might drop some litter or step on a wildflower by mistake. Don't get me wrong, you'd get a stern ticking-off from a Ranger and be made to pick up the crisp packet. But really, if you're English, in what world is there an escaped murderer on the loose in the place you've gone to have a nice walk and a picnic?

Here's where Danny Ray Horning comes in. Convicted bank-robber and all-round bad guy, Horning escaped from state prison in Arizona in May 1992, where he was serving four consecutive life sentences for armed robbery and kidnapping. He went to ground in the Arizona back-country, raiding homes and cabins and stealing cars, only emerging to rob another bank, while staying one step ahead of the authorities by using his wilderness survival skills. The longer he evaded captivity, the more he became celebrated as a real-life Rambo and Robin Hood in local newspapers and on TV – despite the fact that he was also a convicted child molester and murder suspect in an ongoing case in California.

By late-June 1992 Horning was the subject of the largest manhunt in Arizona's history, and – running out of options – had come up with a plan to kidnap a family for ransom. After a couple of false starts and botched attempts, he headed for one of America's most popular tourist sites, the Grand Canyon, and promptly went to ground again, biding his time. By now, everyone in Arizona – and large parts of the USA – knew all about the manhunt for the armed and highly dangerous Danny Ray Horning.

Except us, obviously.

The search teams, the helicopters, the sightings, even a close-shave shoot-out and sudden-death disappearance – all were headline news, day after day, on every TV channel and radio station. Yet we had contrived to miss the lot as we motored along western highways living our tourist version of the American Dream.

To be fair to us, we were permanently distracted. Figuring out how America worked was a full-time job, starting at the car rental place, where they gave us an automatic with cruise control. Both of those vehicle facilities were novel concepts for English, cramped-road, stick-shifters, so – entirely reasonably – we made a few circuits of the airport car park to try them out. After five minutes or so, and now up to about twenty-five miles an hour and fairly confident we knew which the correct side of the road was for driving on, a security guard flagged us down, told us off for causing a nuisance and threw us out onto the roaring highway.

Luckily, the car basically seemed to drive itself, which was a good job since the business of keeping it fuelled and on the road caused us no end of consternation ("Why do they call it gas? It's not a gas, it's a liquid?! Crazy Americans!"). In one small town, we pulled in at a garage with an automatic car wash, which we thought would be a fun American thing to do. But because we were British and a bit crap at driving, we misjudged the drive-on-washy-bit, panicked halfway through when the car started rocking alarmingly, and sped out before it was done, fully sudsed and trailing bubbles down the street.

We were also endlessly engaged by the vast landscapes and natural wonders ("Look, a cactus!" – "Is that an actual Roadrunner?"). I can't tell you how big and exciting continental

71

America is to people who come from a small island. England's highest mountain tops out at three thousand feet and you have to climb up it on a stony path; one day, we drove – *drove* – across a mountain pass in the Rockies that was twelve thousand feet high. That's like driving almost halfway up Mount Everest in a family sedan.

By the time we reached Arizona, three weeks or so into our trip, we had knocked the edges off our Englishness and were beginning to relax. Gas/petrol, it was all the same to us. We'd had burgers in diners and Buds in bars. I'd say we were basically American by now.

Sat in a traffic queue for a while as dusk fell, we were looking forward to drinks in the lodge at Grand Canyon Village. We'd come up the road from Flagstaff – the same as Danny Ray, if only we'd known – and the hold-up was frustrating and unexplained, though we assumed it was because the Fourth of July was coming up.

The first we knew of the real reason was when we wound down the window.

"Folks, we're advising everyone to turn back."

By now, Horning had been sighted at various points in Grand Canyon National Park, but he had always managed to slip away. Checkpoints were set, with the thought that he'd probably try to escape by hijack or kidnap, using tourists as cover on America's busiest holiday weekend.

But we had a reservation, and the lodge was just a few miles ahead. We were from out of town, we had nowhere else to go.

Was the officer sure we couldn't just drive on to our accommodation?

"Well, all right. I can't stop you. But may God help you!"

It was all in the intonation.

That wasn't a man saying how disappointed he was to have seen us dropping litter or stepping on an orchid. That was a police officer telling us he was worried something terrible might happen if we didn't listen to him.

Danny Ray Horning was armed and dangerous, had been on the run for six weeks, and had already hijacked at least three vehicles in the last few days, escaping every time. We didn't know that, but we had been told by an US law enforcement officer – with a gun! At an actual American roadblock! – that a very bad man was at large somewhere in the Grand Canyon, looking for a way out. And we treated it as seriously as a British person treats most edicts from authority – oh it can't be that bad, I'm sure it's all fine, as long as we're careful, let's have a cup of tea.

Even so – not quite believing that anything would happen – it was still a long ride through the trees on a dark road to the lodge at the Grand Canyon. A long ride half-expecting a man to emerge from the shadows pointing a gun, but not really, because that would be crazy, what kind of country is this?

The atmosphere at the lodge, when we got there, unmolested, was subdued. There was only a handful of people in the lobby and lounge. Others, doubtless more sensible, had clearly not made the same trip we had – had turned round when offered the chance. We drank a quiet drink and ate a quiet meal, and turned in to bed, listening to the rustle of the wind and the creak of the boards and eventually falling asleep, though never feeling fully reassured that a man who's name we didn't yet know wasn't lurking somewhere outside.

The next day we stood at the canyon viewpoint and marvelled at the grandeur while arguing in a very British way about its relative size and importance.

As a spectacle, the Grand Canyon is too big, too large to appreciate. Does everyone say that? It's almost two hundred and eighty miles long and up to eighteen miles wide in places. Those are crazy numbers for the mind to manage. You don't peer over the edge, at a plummeting rock face that falls to a snaking river – as in the Westerns you've seen and the novels you've read. Instead, you look out over shimmering swathes of graded colours that fall away into an interlocking landscape of bluffs, peaks, table-tops and valleys. It's hard to work out where the edge on the other side is – whether there even is an edge. You try to take in its vast scale and fail miserably.

We peered through some binoculars and took some photos, and then we left on the five-hour drive to Las Vegas, where a phantom escaped convict rather paled into insignificance when confronted with the unrealities that unfold every day in that miraculous city in the desert – where Venice and Camelot, Frank and Elvis, Caravaggio and Elton, all somehow come into sharper view than the river at the bottom of a mile-deep canyon.

That's where my Grand Canyon story might have finished – a not-quite tale of a non-encounter, which I've recounted many times – if I hadn't thought to Google 'escaped convict grand canyon 1992' when I first thought about writing this piece. All I had was an anecdote and half a story, but the internet gave me the rest.

That's when I learned that our escaped convict had a name – Danny Ray Horning – and that Danny Ray was no Rambo or Robin Hood but a thoroughly nasty piece of work; not just a prison escapee but also the chief suspect in an ongoing murder and dismemberment case.

So Danny Ray Horning was a genuinely bad and dangerous man. And two days after we had driven through the roadblocks, into and out of the Grand Canyon, ignoring the police warnings, he emerged from his hiding place somewhere in the forest. He walked up to the viewpoint parking area, pulled his gun and kidnapped two British tourists, and then forced them to drive their rental car out of the park, slipping through the net one more time. Mercifully, that's all he did – eventually tying them to a tree and making a final, short-lived escape before eventually being captured on the fifth of July, 1992, after seven weeks on the run.

Two British tourists. Not us, but two others who probably also thought that things like that just don't happen, it can't be that bad, I'm sure it's all fine, as long as we're careful, let's have a cup of tea.

And that is where my newly minted Grand Canyon story might have finished, except for one more odd coincidence. Down at the bottom of one of the online stories I used for source material about Danny Ray Horning was a link to another newspaper story in a publication from my English hometown of Huddersfield in Yorkshire.

After his capture and re-arrest, Danny Ray had subsequently been convicted of murder and sentenced to death. While on death row in San Quentin State Prison in California he had struck up a pen-pal relationship with a retired teacher from Huddersfield, who – the *Huddersfield Daily Examiner* was reporting in 2013 – believed in his innocence and was planning on visiting him.

After that, the trail runs cold and my story comes to an end.

California announced a moratorium on the death penalty in 2019, so Danny Ray Horning remains – as far as I know – in prison.

The Grand Canyon endures, its unfathomable gulf widening and deepening, grain by grain, year by year. Looking back at the photos I took on that July holiday weekend thirty years ago, I still can't decide if it's the most impressive natural wonder I've ever visited, or the most over-rated.

America, however, continues to be the most recognisable yet strangest place on the planet, a land where Arizona and Huddersfield can collide against all the odds, where escaped convicts do hide in the trees, and where police officers should probably be taken at their word.

A walk away from heartbreak in England

THE CURE, I thought, for a broken heart would be a good long walk. So I took a nine-hour bus ride to Cornwall late one summer, got off in Bude and started on down the South West Coast Path. Turn left, keep the sea on the right, mourn a lost love, relinquish an old life, contemplate a new one – that was the general plan and it must have worked because here I am, years later, heart fully mended and new life most definitely lived.

However, when I say "plan," that's a very specific word for what was a very loosely conceived idea. Head to the Cornish coast, start walking, stop when I felt a bit better. If I'm honest, that was about the gist of it. There might have been some notion of Byronesque tramping, wind in my flowing locks, seeking pleasure in the pathless woods and rapture on the lonely shore, that sort of thing. At the very least I thought I could tire myself out during the day and drink myself to sleep at night in cheery inns full of shanty-singing fishermen in cable-knit sweaters.

I could have been better prepared, is what I think I'm saying.

For a start, I wasn't really a walker back then. I mean, I'd been on walks obviously. You can't be English and not have to go on a walk at some point. When you're younger, your parents make you do it on Sundays "to get some fresh air," like that's something a teenager wants, and you're introduced to words related to the activity of walking – fun, interesting, exciting – that bear no relation to the emotions you are currently experiencing in a mud-filled swamp of a farmer's field.

"It's not cold, it's bracing" you're told, as the sleet slashes against your face and your inadequate boots fill with a rising tide of farmyard slurry. Later, you inflict the same terrible outings on your own children, prising their fingers from the consoles, forcing their feet into wellies that don't fit, ignoring the shrieks of protest and the threats that they'll call Child Services themselves.

"I had to do it, so you have to do it. We're English. Now get your boot out of the mud and let's go."

It's probably buried deep in our anglo-DNA, a double helix that twists "a nice cup of tea" around "a good country walk". Pointless meanders in random bits of countryside; hikes up disappointing hills in driving rain; circuits of stately home gardens under leaden skies; rambles to places of no distinction. This is mostly what English people think of as walking and I can tell you now that it's no preparation for tackling England's longest and toughest footpath.

I'd been on holiday to the Lake District a few times – again, if you're English, you have to, it's the law – but, on account of the mountains and the lakes, you can never walk very far while you're there. A few miles in a day in a relentless drizzle – again, legal requirement – up, down and around, and that's your lot. It's not so much long-distance walking as high-altitude trudging, and when the clouds lift – approximately twice a year – you can generally see exactly where you set off from, about a mile and several hours below.

The South West Coast Path, though, is six hundred and thirty miles long, one single footpath tracing the extravagantly contoured coasts of Somerset, Devon, Cornwall and Dorset. You can't see where you're going and you can't see where you've been. That's what you call a decent walk. That also seemed like both a metaphor and a better bet for a distracted man; rather less chance, I thought, of falling off a mountain while examining the wreckage of my life. Simply follow the path, one foot in front of another, acquire some inner peace and go home again.

I bought an official guidebook to the route, where I discovered a slightly disconcerting fact. Those six hundred and thirty miles don't breeze along gentle paths, mild slopes and grassy swards; they buck like broncos up cliffs and down coves, crossing rocky shores and climbing sheer steps. They grab your feet by the throat, if such a thing is possible, and let them know that they are in for one hell of a pounding. Also, walking the whole thing would take eight weeks, which was precisely seven weeks and six days more than I had ever walked in one go before.

Still, the Byron in me did like the sound of North Cornwall – rugged, wild and uplifting according to the book. And I figured I could make it at least as far as Land's End, mainland Britain's most southwesterly point, which seemed like a suitable place to stand on the cliffs, say goodbye to an old life and welcome a new one.

Bude's a surf town. Tennyson – Alfred, Lord of Bondi – wrote of its "thundering shores" before jumping on his Malibu longboard, but I didn't see anything of it, arriving late and leaving early the next morning. Starting the walk, I was not what you'd call refreshed, having spent the night in a lumpy bed in the sort of traditional English B&B that gives solitary confinement a bad name. Breakfast, I was informed the night before, was served from seven-forty-five am, and I am never reassured by the sort of establishment that makes you choose what you're going to eat for breakfast before you've even had your dinner. It's a fried egg and some bacon, how much notice do you need to cook them? I toddled down the next morning at five to eight and there indeed was breakfast, a Full English, set on a table with my room number on it. Set there on a table "at" and not "from" seven forty-five in fact, and – ten minutes in and congealing – no longer in tip-top eating condition.

This path was not going to walk itself, so I shivved the jailer and broke out of chokey – well, handed back the key in an offhand manner to suggest mild disappointment while thanking the B&B owner profusely in the British way for such a delightful stay. Cornwall awaited.

For the first couple of miles, frankly I wondered what all the fuss had been about. The path was gentle and true, along a grassy swathe above Bude's beaches, and I bounded and zipped while getting used to the weight of the backpack. At this rate, I could knock off six hundred and thirty miles in about three days. Bude's outskirts turned into the long and impressive sweep of Widemouth Bay, and we might as well address the vagaries of Cornish pronunciation at this point. Basically, ignore the way anything is spelled and have a random go at a selection of sounds and emphases. So here I was at Wid-muth Bay, with Mousehole (pronounced Mowzle), Pelynt (Plint) and Fowey (Foy) to come. If I didn't get lost it wasn't going to be for the want of trying.

Once across the sands at Widemouth, the path began to climb and then plunge across a series of rollercoaster valleys and clifftops that pretty much continued for the next two weeks. This was clearly what the guidebook had meant by "Terrain: challenging and strenuous" and I pushed on increasingly slowly, inching out of narrow, rocky clefts and climbing up steep, stepped paths onto exposed promontories that offered a brief respite before the next knee-cracking descent. The views out to the Atlantic were magnificent at times and I dropped the backpack now and again to catch a breath, but it was extremely hard going and this was just the first day.

I cheered up on reaching Crackington Haven and who wouldn't? Excellent name and with a pub overlooking a dramatic, enclosed cove for a well-earned pint. Leafing through the guidebook at this point, there was good news and bad news. I'd already walked ten miles, which seemed like a cause for celebration, another pint, thank you landlord, don't mind if I do. But due to an administrative error it seemed that I still had another six miles to go to Boscastle, because I had looked in the wrong column and thought that I was walking sixteen kilometres on my first day. I wasn't, it was sixteen miles and now I'd had two pints, which strictly speaking is two more than you'd want to have if you were already knackered and now had to negotiate some more challenging and strenuous terrain.

I wasn't thinking much about my broken heart at this point, I can tell you that. So I suppose the walk was already doing its job.

I limped into Boscastle later that afternoon and trudged down the hillside path to the narrow neck of the harbour. The village was clearly popular with tourists but seemed to me to be a rather intimidating place, with old houses and cottages set around the confluence of two gushing rivers. When clouds scudded over the skirting hills, the light suddenly disappeared in the narrow lanes. If you've heard of Boscastle at all, it's probably because it was almost washed away in devastating floods in 2004. Having been there in that deep gully, it's not hard to imagine the speed of the water as it thundered down off the hills, washing vehicles into the harbour and cutting off the village for days.

I stayed overnight at Boscastle's youth hostel, an old stone house right on the harbour under the rocks. That first day's walking had taken its toll. The backpack was clearly heavier than when I had started – I suspect small children had filled it with rocks at Crackington Haven – and it was difficult to distinguish between aches. I was just one big pulled muscle. The inside of my right big toe was already badly blistered, and I had to pop it with the prongs of a fork from the dining room so I could add a plaster to stop it chafing any further. If that was you twirling spaghetti later, sorry about that. I staggered to the nearest pub, dozed over a deep-fried meal of something with chips and headed back for a good night's sleep.

If you'd like to recreate the experience of occupying a male dorm bed in a hiker's hostel, then here's what you do. Invite a particularly hairy men's rugby team for a sleepover in your attic. Ensure that they have all drunk several pints of strong Cornish beer called things like Nob Rocket and Old Gussett and then establish two rotas: one for going to bed loudly, two at a time, on the hour up until midnight while switching the lights on and off and shouting "Shush"; and the second for clambering down off the bunks in the pitch black to go the toilet muttering "Ouch" and "Bollocks." For the full effect, set various alarm calls for any time from six in the morning onwards. Also, make sure you have jumbled up everyone's backpacks while they're asleep so that you awake to the frantic sound of a hairy prop forward going through your pack looking for his missing pants.

It was, in short, a noisy, windy, rumbling, restless, fart-filled night. Again, sorry about that everyone.

The next day's walking was no easier, a slightly shorter hack to Port Isaac that was flagged up in advance as "particularly challenging." But once I'd accepted that I was now simply a large, mobile ache on legs, I slowly grew into the punishing descents and ascents. The coastal and seaward views were never anything less than stunning, and the weather was a revelation. For someone who had grown up in Yorkshire and done most of their walking thus far in the English Lake District – motto: Of course it's raining, why do you think we've got lakes? – a Cornish summer of blue skies and bright sun seemed like a category error. No one ever mentioned this when they were handing out places to live. It was actually warm in August, hot even. Butterflies danced in the gullies as I climbed, and seabirds dipped and swooped in the thermals off the cliff edges.

At Tintagel, tourism briefly intervened again as day-trippers swirled around the craggy headland where King Arthur was born. It's a romantic site, fully signed up to the myths and legends ascribed to it, but I walked on through. The part of me that has got a history degree didn't stop, because Arthur probably never existed and, if he did, he was just a sixth-century Welsh prince with no magic sword who almost certainly didn't live in Cornwall. But mostly I didn't stop because I'd never have started again. I was beginning to realise that my legs only kept working if you gave them no time to think and no options. What did they think this was, a holiday? One in front of the other, fellas, that's all they needed to know.

I did pause a little later for what I decided should become a daily occurrence – a pint of beer in an amusingly named beachside hamlet. Move over Crackington Haven and hello Trebarwith Strand, which sounded like it should be the name of a Cornish secret agent or a tool you might use on a building site ("That looks tricky, pass me the trebarwith strand and keep well clear."). I had a pint of Jolly Knee Trembler on a terrace outside the Port William pub and consulted the trail guidebook for the next leg to Port Isaac, seven miles away.

I almost hadn't bought the guidebook. How hard could the South West Coast Path be to follow? You literally just needed to keep the sea on your right and walk along the coast. Also, the only other coastal hiking guide I had ever purchased turned out to be a dud of the highest order. Once, on the Algarve in Portugal for a few days, a friend and I had bought a copy of a walking guide that shall remain nameless because I can't afford to get sued. It was a translation from a European language into English, presumably by someone who spoke neither language, for the walking instructions were largely impenetrable – "By the second fence in advance of the junction insomuch we proceed westerly and so we go on" was a typical sentence. That soon became a running joke – choosing a random direction at a junction while declaiming the cheery phrase "And so we go on!", before backtracking ten minutes later and trying the alternative. Even ignoring the instructions and following the hand-drawn maps, the routes were equally baffling. We'd start off on a glorious stretch of the Algarve coast, with a golden beach and shimmering rock formations ahead, and within five minutes we'd be sent inland over a barbed-wire fence into litter-filled scrub. On one memorable walk we circled an entire sewage and water-treatment facility on a raised concrete path above purple foaming water; occasionally we'd catch cries of laughter and enjoyment carried on the gentle breeze from the nearby coastal path. I looked up the book's reviews on Amazon later, which are amusingly irate and very heavily weighted towards the one- and two-star end of the spectrum. It's still for sale by the way; you are most welcome.

My Cornish footpath guide though was proving invaluable. Ignoring user error, it had been so far infallible, telling me which bits were hard going and which bits I was going to enjoy. Yes, the directions never amounted to much more than "Keep the sea on your right," but when it said that the upcoming section was "especially long and difficult" I saw no reason to doubt it. As it was also holding out the promise of "harbourside pubs," plural, I put my best foot forward, proceeding southerly and so we go on.

Port Isaac was all that was promised, more attractive than Boscastle and set around another harbour, offering beer, seafood and ice cream in equal measure. Had I only known at the time, this would have the very place to break out the knitwear and start a shanty band with the wind-chapped fishing lads from the local pub. Someone beat me to it, because Port Isaac's Fishermen's Friends later signed a million-pound record contract and appeared at Glastonbury and I am in no way miffed about that missed opportunity.

Another day's hiking put me in the fishing port of Padstow, where – true story – I remembered it was my birthday and treated myself to seared tuna in Rick Stein's restaurant. Then it was on around jutting headlands and sheltered inlets, and across wide sandy beaches, for the long pull south towards Newquay, the first town I'd seen in almost a week.

By now, the walk had become a rhythmic part of my life. I was sleeping better – even in hostels – getting up early, eating enormous fried breakfasts and then hiking for most of the day. Sea on the right, one foot in front of the other, mile after mile, day after day. I nodded and said hello to passing walkers, steamed on past dawdling families, and sat on bouncy grass to eat sandwiches, overlooking the vast Atlantic. I lay with my head close to gorse and heather and watched scudding clouds and diving kittiwakes. I read about tin miners and Iron Age villages, trailed my fingers in rockpools and, now and again, took off my boots and walked into the surf, feeling the sand trickle away from my toes as the waves receded.

I suppose you might call this healing. At the time I just figured that I was filling the days at least, while getting fitter. If intrusive thoughts made their presence known at any point, I really only had to wait for the next brutal ascent with a weighty backpack to send them on their way.

It was forty miles and another three days to St Ives, which was full of artists carting easels around and generally making nuisances of themselves at every delightful viewpoint. I stopped more times than was strictly necessary, got myself painted into some landscapes, and then pushed on another twenty-five miles to Land's End, where I had originally expected some kind of cathartic release, or at least a bit of a sit-down.

In the end, I enjoyed neither. I was a long-distance walker now. The trail, not the destination, was becoming the point. It had been over a hundred and thirty miles since Bude and the best part of two weeks on a single path, footstep after footstep, sea on the right. Land's End, like Tintagel before it, was rich in romance and history, an end in itself for many, but not for me. When all's said and done, it's just another headland, another ocean view, another wild Atlantic look-out – and this one was crawling with tourists because you can drive right there, park up and exit by the gift shop. I tipped my hat to the southwestern tip of mainland Britain, vowed also to go to John O'Groats one day in the far northeast (still not been) and walked on.

I kept going for another two days, heading around the wild capes beyond Land's End before cutting northeast towards Penzance. There was a surprise at Porthcurno, a perfect outdoor amphitheatre, carved into the cliff-edge rocks, and my usual pint of beer (Moist Badger) in the usual humorously named village (Mousehole). Then suddenly, a couple of miles beyond Mowzle, the footpath did something most unexpected: it stopped being strenuous and challenging and turned into a nice, flat, tarmacked road as it traced around the harbour of Newlyn and ran into the town of Penzance.

I stayed the night and did the maths the next morning. From Bude to Penzance, I had walked exactly a hundred and fifty miles. That seemed like an achievement. The question was, did I need to keep going? Physically, I was broken in by now and up to the challenge. My feet and shoulders no longer hurt; my heart, I figured, would take care of itself.

On reflection, I thought I was probably done with the South West Coast Path and there, in lovely, sunny Penzance, on a bright morning by the quayside, the path was finally done with me. One day perhaps, there would be time and reason to tackle the remaining four hundred and eighty miles, but for now that was enough.

I toasted my decision with a few pints of Rabbit Strangler and caught the bus back the next day – heading home to a different life than I had originally planned but which would be just fine as long as I kept one foot in front of the other, sea on the right.

A dive on the reef in Egypt

"AND ONE MORE thing," says Callum, the scuba-diving instructor, "I don't want to hear anyone calling these flippers and goggles. They're fins and masks. This isn't splash time. It's serious stuff."

We all look suitably chastened. Callum looks like he was chiselled from marble, had life breathed into him by the Gods, poured into a pair of swim-shorts, spray-tanned and then plonked poolside. He's already shown us how ridiculously long he can hold his breath underwater – weighted down, he lay still on the bottom, arms folded on his chest in repose, for what seemed like about an hour. If you didn't know better, you'd say he was asleep. Perhaps it's some sort of higher-level deity skill and he actually was asleep? Anyway, if Callum says they're called fins and masks, then that's good enough for us.

"But Callum," says one brave soul brandishing a snorkel, "what's this called then?"

"A snorkel, mate," says Callum.

We all roll our eyes at the heretic. Snorkel. Durr. Obviously. Callum has spoken.

It's the first morning on the learn-to-dive course at Hurghada on the Red Sea. In four days' time I'll be a qualified diver with a PADI (Professional Association of Diving Instructors) certificate to prove it. That seems hard to believe, given that until ten minutes ago I didn't know the correct name for the flippy things I have on my feet. But Callum seems confident and is already running through some other stuff that he thinks we should know.

The things you breathe through, for example. There's the regulator, or air mouthpiece, for starters, which is the bit of kit that delivers oxygen from the tank to your mouth, plus another bit of mouthpiece-and-hose kit known as an octopus which Callum describes as a "back-up air source."

We gloss over the potential requirement for a back-up air source. Back-up. Substitute. Replacement. That eventuality – running out of air – is not something anyone really wants to think about. We just want to go diving on the reef and see the pretty fish.

Then there's the BCD, which looks like a jetpack but turns out to be an inflatable jacket (in fact, a "buoyancy control device"). If you're on the surface and sinking, you can blow into the little tube and fill it up with a bit more air. Again. If you're sinking. Let's not ask.

Fins, mask, snorkel, we know all about.

Now can we go diving, Callum, and see the pretty fish?

It seems not.

We take everything off again and spend the next two days either in the classroom or the hotel pool learning about the

Byzantine complexities of scuba diving. Apparently, it's not just a matter of hooking yourself up to an oxygen tank, sticking on some goggles, sorry Callum, masks, and jumping in.

In the classroom there are PowerPoint presentations about diving depths, oxygen pressure, buoyancy calculations and the human anatomy. Interesting facts are learned. Your lungs are basically big inflatable pockets. Breathe out and deflate and you sink. Breathe in and you rise. Information such as this features in a multiple-choice exam, without passing which you can't continue any further. Callum – patiently – sees to it that everyone passes.

Some alarming facts are also learned. Did you know, for instance, that blood appears green under water? We did not, and we all file that one away with the back-up air source info. What could befall you – attached to a tank of high-pressure oxygen under ten metres of open ocean – that you need to be aware of the colour of your own spilled blood? Callum, wisely, does not say and we do not ask. We just tick the box that says "green" and hope we'll never need to know.

In the early mornings, while the regular hotel guests are still circling the breakfast buffet, Callum puts us through our paces in the shallow family pool. We get used to "buddying up," helping each other put on and check the kit that is going to let us dive, swim and breathe. The water in the pool comes up to our chests at most and we bob around in the bulky jackets trying to remember the PowerPoint slide about achieving neutral buoyancy. Funny how the exact hue of your spurting underwater blood can easily be recalled; buoyancy calculations, not so much.

Regulators in, masks on, all sounding now like Darth Vader having a swimming lesson, we drop below the surface for the first time.

What godlike trickery is this? All hail Callum, bless him, for he has been telling the truth all along. You can breathe under water! Fair enough, in the shallow pool, you could also get off your knees, stand up and breathe out of the water too. Octopus, schmoctopus, sticking your head back out of the water is more our kind of back-up air source. But we get the point. This is how it's going to work when we're out in the ocean. Pretty fish here we come.

Although not quite yet.

For a start, none of us is actually doing any of what might ordinarily be recognised as breathing. Instead, there is lots of panicked gasping, each of us convinced that the air will run out at any minute. How much can be in those tanks anyway? A couple of balloons full? Half an air-bed's worth? I'm sucking up mine big time while I can and, looking around at my wide-eyed, mask-misted colleagues, so is everyone else.

Callum sits quietly on the floor of the pool with his arms crossed against his chest while we all bounce around hyperventilating, a metre or so under the surface. It's all highly entertaining for the hotel guests who have finished breakfast and are beginning to stake out positions around the pool.

Gradually we learn to trust the tech and calm down. Our heart rates slow and Callum begins the underwater lessons.

When we surface ten minutes or so later, he makes a point of showing us the oxygen gauges. Red-faced and buzzing, we've used up half our air supply with our get-it-while-we-can, fast-breathing antics. Callum, on the other hand, has gone the full Zen Master and got through only about five percent of his air. He could probably live down there without too much trouble. I can see us all making the same mental note to self – stick close to Callum, the boy's always got air to spare.

By the end of the second day, we have done several seemingly impossible things on the bottom of a swimming pool under Callum's careful supervision. One involves taking your mask off, letting it fill with water, putting it back on again and then purging it of water, while – and I can't stress this enough – you are still under the actual water. That clearly shouldn't work but, thanks to some sort of magic and trickery, it does. There's another bit where the mystery of the octopus is solved, since it turns out that the back-up air source can be used to help another diver in trouble, and we all have a go at breathing through each other's spare tube. Again, under the water, like we're proper divers and everything.

We also address the future problem of getting out of the boat and into the water. There's the cool, grown-up way, which involves sitting on the edge, back to the water, and doing a backwards roll while holding on to your face-mask and regulator so that nothing pops out when you hit the water. This is harder than it looks, even in a swimming pool. It results in bewildered novice divers trying to right themselves with flailing arms and fins; it results in much water up noses; it results, frankly, in chaos.

Luckily, there's a second method, which requires nothing more complicated than springing with one giant step, scissor-legged, off the edge, after which you just bob about the right way up, waiting for instructions. We'll take option B then, thanks very much.

Callum has one final test and we don't like the sound of it one bit. We're to kneel on the floor of the pool and he's going to turn off our oxygen supply from the tank "just briefly, so you can see what it feels like." You're all right Callum, thanks, we think we have a pretty shrewd idea what not being able to breathe under water will feel like. But it's part of the course and we all have to comply, so one at a time we sink to the floor while Callum turns off our oxygen.

It doesn't go brilliantly well.

The underwater diver's sign for everything being all right is to connect the thumb and forefinger into a circle and hold the other fingers up straight behind. It means "I'm OK" or, held in front of someone else, "Are you OK?"

Giving a thumb's up, on the other hand, means that you want to go back up to the surface. And while here in the pool we could just stand up, Callum is training us to communicate effectively while ten metres under the water. So every time a flustered trainee diver feels the air die in their tank, sees Callum give the "Are you OK?" signal and responds with a hasty thumbs-up, they find themselves hauled to their feet and reminded that if they do that in the ocean their dive will be over. No more pretty fish.

Out on the dive-boat on the morning of the third day, the nerves kick in.

Until now we've spent more time in a hotel conference room than under the water. But we're currently chugging away from the dockside of one of Egypt's biggest Red Sea resorts. A breeze ruffles the aquamarine water – disappointingly not red, we all check – and, in the distance, the curved reef walls form a sheltered pool in which we'll make our first open-water dive. We've learned the skills and done the drills, and the water is a comforting thirty degrees Celsius, but there comes a point – quite soon – at which we're going to have to giant-stride or back-roll into the water; at which we're going to have to trust Callum, trust the equipment, trust ourselves and submit to the deep.

Not really bothered about the pretty fish to be honest at this point – it's more about keeping the buffet breakfast down.

Callum has a final piece of technical diving information for us. It wasn't in the exam, but to be fair to him you can see why he might have kept it back until now.

"Guys, the regulator" – the bit you breathe through – "needs to stay in your mouth at all times, just like we practiced. But don't worry if you feel sick. They've been designed so that you can vomit through them under water."

We will laugh about this later in the hotel bar, as we review the day's dives and celebrate the fact that we all made it back in one piece. We'll order a first beer and toast Callum, who will slope off after an hour and warn us not to have too many drinks because we're diving again tomorrow.

We'll recall the feeling as we first put our heads in the warm water of the Red Sea and caught flashes of primary colours flitting beneath our flippers, sorry Callum, fins. There they were, the pretty clownfish, trumpet fish, butterfly fish and parrotfish, but no one – not even Callum – had ever said how vivid and bright they would be. They were also startlingly large and close, and we'll cast our minds back to the classroom session where we learned that because of relative air and mask-lens density, everything under water appears twenty-five percent larger and closer than it really is. Which turned out not to be a great deal of help or reassurance, we'll agree, when we spotted that reef shark, forgot everything we had learned ("reef shark – small, shy, unthreatening") and gasped uncontrollably through about a year's worth of oxygen before Callum had gathered and calmed his scattering flock.

We will order more beers and chalk off the other species seen – moray eel, turtle, lobster, stingray, snapper, barracuda. Like three-year-olds at the zoo getting excited by the pile of leaves outside the lion's enclosure, we'll prompt each other about more mundane highlights too – that bit of old anchor! That rock with the hole!

We'll marvel at the three-dimensional world we explored, where even our ungainly movements seemed balletic and graceful. We'll talk about how we stuck closely to each other – buddy to buddy, barely out of fingertip reach, for fear of getting separated – until gradually, minute by minute, we relaxed into the water, lulled by the all-encompassing experience. We'll remember Callum picking up shells and stones from the white sand seabed, and parting fronds and pointing into crevices on the coral reef wall. We'll smile and laugh at the sheer, impossible joy of it all.

We'll slap backs and say we did it, and write the first entries in our diving logbooks. And we'll order even more beers and stay up later than we should, because if we're hungover tomorrow for our second day of open-water diving, we can always be sick through our regulators.

We'll do all this later, after our first dive. But now there's just silence as the engine is cut and the first pair of buddies comes to the edge of the boat. We watch them check each other's gear one final time and shuffle forwards. We hold our breaths and wait our turn.

"Ready to dive?", says Callum.

A holiday in hell in England

THERE'S A FAMOUS old English saying, dating originally from the seventeenth century, that's pretty clear about the three places it really doesn't recommend for a weekend break.

"From Hell, Hull and Halifax, may the Good Lord deliver us."

As it happens, I've been to Hell. It's a village on the Trondheim railway line in Norway and an obligatory stop for postcards, given that there are pictures for sale of Hell freezing over in winter. Who wouldn't want one of those? It's fun to get an ice cream too and eat it by the station sign, for obvious reasons. Hell, in short, isn't. It's quite nice, if you like middle-of-nowhere Scandinavian villages.

I've also been to the old Victorian textile town of Halifax in northern England, many times, but it's literally too close to home to write about. It's only a few miles from Huddersfield in West Yorkshire, where I grew up, and it has the same Pennine grittiness and lack of attraction. When J.B. Priestley drove around England in the 1930s for his book, *English Journey*, he gave Halifax both barrels, describing it as grim, craggy, piercingly cold and yet, despite all this, "more interesting than Leeds." Priestley was from neighbouring Bradford and therefore biased, so it's probably fairer to say that Halifax isn't without charm, and people doubtless live perfectly pleasant lives there, but no one would choose to have a holiday in Halifax.

In case this comes over as a bit churlish, I ought to say that I have a routine at book readings where I introduce my travel memoirs by saying that – born in Takoradi, Ghana, raised in Huddersfield, Yorkshire – I don't really come from anywhere. However, there are two places that have shaped me. One is a small, non-descript town that few have ever heard of, with no tourist attractions and little reason to visit. And the other is Takoradi.

You really have to be there, but – substitute Halifax for Huddersfield – you get the idea.

That said, I read a recent newspaper report about the post-Covid hopes for Yorkshire tourism, in which the Chief Executive was quoted as saying, "People are looking to discover those places that maybe were on a bucket list but they'd never got round to, *like Selby, Barnsley and Doncaster.*" My italics, as they very much say.

I don't know which I like best: the idea that the Yorkshire towns of Selby, Barnsley and Doncaster were ever on anyone's bucket list; or the thought of stray foreign tourists turning up on the say-so of an apparently authoritative newspaper article, which is entirely the sort of thing I have done in the past. On the strength of an effusive restaurant review, I once travelled all the way to Taranto in Apulia in southern Italy – "An important commercial and naval port with well-developed steel and iron foundries, oil refineries, chemical works, naval shipyards and food-processing factories," if you are unfamiliar with its attractions. I did at least get some seafood *antipasti* and a decent grilled fish meal in Taranto, while the blazing Adriatic sun shone over the oil derricks. My guess is you'll find that a tougher proposition in Selby, Barnsley or Doncaster.

All of which jollity leaves us with Hull, a river port and city on the eastern fringes of Yorkshire. Named after the minor river it sits on, and blown by chill winds from the North Sea, it's closer to Amsterdam than it is to London – J.B. Priestley's opinion (and I'm warming to him now) was that "unless you should happen to be going to one of the Baltic countries, Hull is out of your way." It's the very definition of end-of-the-line, and is the final place from which the Good Lord should deliver us.

Even if you're British, chances are you've never been to Hull. If you're not from the UK, you've probably never heard of it. It has – shall we say – a reputation, and one that goes back centuries if the "Hell, Hull and Halifax" line is any guide. That phrase is from a poem, the *Beggars' Litany*, and reflects the commonly held view in the seventeenth century that Hull and Halifax were particularly unfortunate places for villains, vagrants, miscreants and ne'er-do-wells. All the evidence suggests that you really didn't want to get caught doing something you shouldn't in either town. In Halifax, the punishment for even minor offences was the "Halifax Gibbet", a sort of early guillotine; in Hull you could expect to be tied to a post in the murky river and left to drown, or turned over to the Navy press gang and flogged to work onboard a ship.

The following centuries did little to rescue its reputation. Poor old 'Ull – the local accent can't even run to a capital H. A city forever on the edge, stuck to the mud of the Humber estuary, bombed and blitzed as badly as London during World War II, dependent on a declining fishing industry, and then abandoned by successive governments as austerity bit deep and then carried on biting. It even went straight in at number one in *Crap Towns: The Fifty Worst Places to Live in the UK*, an actual 2003 publication that caused a stink in all the places it maligned (and much hilarity elsewhere, obviously).

Given all that, why would you go? Reputation's a bitch.

But to a travel writer, Hull should not present a challenge. There's history there in abundance, while finding things to write about and making them sound interesting is what I do for a living. Travel writing doesn't always have to be about the exotic, the foreign, the far away. We should be able to celebrate the next-door and near-at-hand, whose stories are just as engaging and valuable. And Hull is only close to home for me. For you, who knows, that single-syllable destination may be impossibly distant and alluring, somewhere to read about and dream of visiting one day.

Even more philosophically, I'm prepared to think that there's something in G.K. Chesterton's famous quotation about travel.

"The whole object of travel," he wrote, "is not to set foot on foreign land; it is at last to set foot on one's own country as a foreign land."

By which I think he meant us to try and understand our own Hulls and Halifaxes; to see them through the eyes of others; to appreciate their mysteries in the same way we do those of Hong Kong or Havana. It shouldn't be hard to do justice to a place like Hull, to craft a story about it that will resonate with others. I've never found a place yet that doesn't have something to recommend it.

And on the face of things, Hull has plenty going for it. I used to visit now and then, back in the day, to cover it for the *Rough Guide to England*. That was already some accolade – Halifax and Huddersfield certainly were never included in the guide, and other overlooked towns and cities were often so outraged by their omission that I was regularly called to appear on local radio to be harangued by apoplectic presenters.

"What's wrong with Smelltown?" they'd demand. "Call yourself a guidebook? Why aren't you covering our Paper Bag Museum? Have you ever even been to the Municipal Abattoir, it's the fifth-widest in England you know?"

By way of contrast, Hull's tourist office was so surprised by the positive coverage it received that my choicest phrases extolling its virtues appeared in the local paper. "Saintly Writer Deserves Knighthood" I believe was the headline. If I'd have made myself known in the city centre, I'd probably have been hoisted shoulder high by cheering townsfolk.

Let's start with the people, because in my experience they are generally funny, generous and welcoming, and not just because they can't believe that they've spotted a tourist. Obviously, the "locals are friendly" trope is a bit lazy of me as a travel writer, so I'd also like to highlight their bluntness. My favourite Hull Twitter person – provoked by one of those random question-threads, "Describe your Twitter feed in five words or fewer" – simply tweeted "Mostly bollocks and swearing."

This down-to-earth obstreperousness is nothing new, by the way. In the English Civil War, Hull declared for Parliament and defied the King, which is an even bigger deal than it might at first appear, given that Hull's official name – bestowed by royal charter in 1299 – is Kingston upon Hull. Kingston, the "king's town", basically locked its gates and told the Royalist soldiers to stuff off.

Daniel Defoe had Robinson Crusoe set sail from Hull, the Yorkshire weather behaving exactly as expected, with his ship no sooner out on the Humber "than the wind began to blow and the sea to rise in a most frightful manner." Here's the thing though. Eventually shipwrecked on a tropical island for twenty-eight years – sun, sand, palm trees, his own private fiefdom – Crusoe has one overriding regret: "Had I the sense to return to Hull, I had been happy."

Hull has moral grit, as the birthplace of William Wilberforce, the man who put a stop to the British slave trade. It's the cultured city that erected a statue of a poet – Philip Larkin – in its railway station and then brought one of his most noted poems to life by scattering giant sculpted toads across its streets and public spaces. (Larkin, being a misery guts of the highest order, didn't really go out of his way to return the favour. He was librarian at the University of Hull for many years, but the best that he could offer by way of praise for his adopted home city was "It's nice and flat for cycling.")

It's the musical hometown of David Bowie's Spiders from Mars – yes indeed, Bowie's backing band was from Hull. Who produced the *Ziggy Stardust* album and played guitar and piano on Lou Reed's seminal "Perfect Day"? Mick Ronson of Hull, that's who – once a local Parks and Rec gardener, whose memorial guitar sculpture now stands in one of the city gardens he used to tend. The Housemartins later called their debut album *London 0 Hull 4*, in case you were in any doubt about what they think of Down South Up North.

Hull is the city with enough emotional intelligence to make its most striking monument not one to royalty or politicians but to its lost, drowned trawlermen. Its most recognisable public artwork isn't a Banksy, perish the thought – it's a rough caricature of an upturned bird, feet sticking into the sky, that was originally painted on a corrugated dockside shed. Ask anyone in Hull about "Dead Bod", they'll tell you the full story. The only place outside London that has hosted art's Turner Prize? Hull. The UK's City of Culture in 2017? You got it.

You're going to need more than this though, I know. You're going to need sights and attractions, so you should probably start with a drive over the spectacular, one-and-a-half-mile long Humber Bridge, England's answer to San Francisco's Golden

Gate. It spans the wide, muddy Humber estuary and, when it was built in the 1980s, was the longest single-span road suspension bridge in the world. It's down to number eleven now (the Golden Gate is a disappointing eighteenth by the way), but it is the longest one in the world that can be crossed on foot, which seems like something that an adventurous tourist might want to do. You would have to be pretty adventurous, mind, since the bridge doesn't really go anywhere – or rather it crosses to the wilds of north Lincolnshire, which amounts to the same thing.

The city planners obviously got their eye in with the bridge and thought, right, what other big, inappropriate showstopper can we bestow upon Hull? It's the only explanation for the supersized shopping mall that overlooks the marina, like they thought it was Monte Freakin' Carlo or something. On a sparkling blue day, with the sun glinting on the spinnakers – is that a thing? – and a takeaway non-dairy flat white from Thieving Harry's, you could imagine yourself a thousand miles south, sizing up your next yacht, before breakfast with your venture-capitalist mates.

Keep heading down towards the river and you'll eventually bump into the world-class aquarium known as The Deep, which features both massive sharks and baby penguins, though not in the same tank, that would be mad. The city museums – excellent, without exception – are all free. One of them contains the oldest ball in Britain, from the thirteenth century, and if that's not worth the journey I don't know what is.

Meanwhile, down on Humber Street, which just used to be a run of old, abandoned fruit and veg warehouses, there are now artisan chocolatiers, cafés with avocado toast, fancy restaurants and a contemporary art gallery. In Trinity Market, there's a pop-up food space where you can grab Sicilian *arancini* and a single-estate coffee, though if you want a real local delicacy ask for "chip spice" on your chips. No one else in Britain has ever heard of this spicy flavouring for fries; in Hull, it's considered a separate food group and lauded for its life-enhancing properties.

What there isn't so much of, however, is what was once Hull's pride and glory – a medieval, Georgian and Victorian streetscape that rivalled that of the far more celebrated York. The city was rich and prosperous for centuries. It traded directly with the Low Countries, the Baltic states and Scandinavia; it was an important whaling port; it sent steamers to the New World. Its trawlers formed the backbone of the English fishing fleet. It coulda had class, coulda been a contender, coulda been somebody, but the bombs ripped out its heart – an extraordinary ninety-five percent of Hull's housing was destroyed or damaged during World War II, as the city's docks and industry, vital to the war effort, were pounded night after night. Just to make the point: York's olde-worlde street of overhanging medieval houses known as The Shambles is famous the world over; yet Hull had an even bigger, better, more impressive one, until it was obliterated by incendiary explosions.

There is a preserved Old Town area, which does at least hint at what might have been. If you ask around, you'll be directed to both England's narrowest window and its greatest street name – The Land of Green Ginger. Again, what more could a visitor want? Meanwhile, the Old Town pubs are like proper English pubs used to be before hipsters brewed beer from socks and sold it in mash-ups of 1950s' diners and Bangkok brothels. They are, in the very best sense, boozers, from sixteenth-century townhouses to tiled Victorian ale-houses – the only other place I know in northern England with a comparable pub landscape is Manchester. The Humber Dock Tavern on the marina, the Minerva on the quayside, Ye Olde White Hart and The George – that's a mini pub crawl right there, and the friendly locals (sorry, travel writer habit) will doubtless point you towards even more.

For all its troubles and detractors, for all the sneering, for all the national indifference to places like Hull, all it takes is for a writer to set foot in it as if it's a foreign land. That's my whole object of travel – to see the difference, appreciate the interest, understand the fascination.

Maybe you'll read this and look beyond the easy generalisations that are made about all sorts of places. Perhaps, one day, you'll even visit Hull, remembering that chapter in a book you once read. If you do, you'll encounter traces of Georgian grandeur, hear Dickensian whispers echoing through the Old Town, and get a teasing glimpse of how high-flying 'Ull once twitched its petticoats – out on the edge, stuck to the mud, but proud as 'ell.

A tale of two satays in Bali

HEAD DOWN A toilet on a palm-fringed Indonesian island – to get all Dickensian on you, I'd say that qualifies as the worst of times, the season of darkness, the winter of despair.

I'd whisked in on an overnight flight, grabbed a taxi at Bali airport and arrived at nearby Kuta Beach just as the sun was setting. Dropped my bag in the guesthouse – cabanas ranged around a small pool – and crossed the road to the nearest restaurant for some chicken skewers and rice.

Plan was – early night, shake off the jet lag, check out Kuta and then decide where to go next on my first trip to Bali.

Plan was not – throw up noisily and energetically, shiver and shake on sopping mattress, and emit strangulated whimperings that carried in the night air.

"Is that a monkey?", said bleary-eyed tourists in neighbouring rooms. "And why is someone waterboarding it? What secrets can it possibly be hiding?"

It was as quick as it was merciless. One minute, laying down the *Lonely Planet* guide and switching off the light. Bit full from the meal, very tired, a little woozy from the flight. Next minute, sat bolt upright, hello, what's this? Nurse, the screens!

By three o'clock in the morning, I was a regular visitor to the tile-floored bathroom. I became familiar with the feel of forearm on porcelain, and when the hand-towel was sodden I wiped my face with a vomit-flecked T-shirt. Between bouts I lay flat on my back under a lacklustre ceiling fan that pushed thick, hot, soup-like air around the room. I'd do a bit of moaning to pass the time and – brought up on *ER* and *Casualty* – check the time between contractions which, who knows why, I thought might be useful information for someone.

By four o'clock, an interesting new development, as explosive diarrhoea made its appearance. Hello, we'd been waiting for you. With George Clooney shouting "Code Brown! Stat!", I made the toilet just in time. It sounded like a bucket of snails being tipped down a well, accompanied by an eye-watering aroma that must have seeped out of the bathroom's louvred windows because every dog in town started yelping.

"I think the monkeys must have escaped," said concerned guests, all now wide awake, "and they've set the dogs on them. I see the sewage truck has broken down too. And who on earth is tipping snails down a well at this time of night?"

By now, I was no longer overly troubled about which end it was coming out of. Only that it either stopped or I died, I'd take either option. Sweat pooled and dripped. I took tiny sips from a bottle of water, cramped up, dashed to the bathroom and gambled on an orifice. I growled, retched, groaned, gagged and snivelled, in no particular order, with the sounds echoing around the bathroom.

"They've recaptured the monkeys everyone. Poor little feckers are being probed with a cattle-prod now."

At some point in the night, all those episodes of *ER* paid off as I remembered that, having sat through fifteen seasons of it, I was basically as good as any doctor. I knew exactly what to do. I ran a few inches of tepid water in the bathtub and climbed in. This finally brought my temperature down, and I lay back on the bed on top of a thin cotton towel and shivered while the water dried on my skin. Close to dawn, with the air the coolest it had been all night, I fell asleep.

When I woke up, the sun was high and guests were splashing in the pool outside, asking if anyone else had heard the overnight noises from the monkey-torture clinic. Aussie backpackers in Billabong boardies slapped past my cabana, giving the bathroom window a wide berth. A guesthouse maid knocked on the locked door at one point, tried the handle and then retreated. I'd need to be getting together a huge wedge of *rupiah* as a pre-emptive tip – danger money really – before I even thought of letting her in the bathroom. I stayed on the bed, sipped more water and just about kept it down.

The next morning, I made it as far as the little covered terrace attached to my room, which overlooked the courtyard and pool. I was repulsed by the thought of food but at the same time ravenous – like John Hurt must have felt after starting dinner with the crew of the *Nostromo* and then suffering the whole alien-out-of-the-stomach episode. Hungry, but then again, under the circumstances, not hungry. What would John Hurt order, I asked myself? I picked up a menu from the plastic table, flagged down a passing employee and plumped for jasmine tea, fingers of dry toast and a boiled egg.

The day unfolded as I moved from hot terrace to cooler room and then back again at dusk, as insects swirled around the light fittings. I stood weakly in the shower, then sat on the bed and read about Bali in the *Lonely Planet* guide – "A mood, an aspiration, a tropical state of mind." Well, if they said so.

It took me three days to recover enough to leave the room properly.

I wandered gingerly into Kuta and down to the beach, past racks of T-shirts and stacked surfboards. It's fair to say that it was not the ideal tonic. The narrow, noisy, dusty lanes were lined with garish gift shops and overbearing vendors hustling hungover tourists. The music from the bars and cafés was too loud, the beach none-too-clean and the zipping mopeds none-too-concerned about cutting up pedestrians. Partying backpackers left the guesthouse when I turned in for the night and came back when I stirred in the morning. I found refuge in a second-hand bookshop on a back lane and whiled away an hour or so each day among the musty shelves of abandoned English-language paperbacks. In a quieter, less touristy restaurant, I moved on to steamed tofu and veg and more hot tea, and hoped for the best.

Better now, after almost a week, I felt that Kuta Beach was not what I was looking for; perhaps Ubud would be.

Bali's cultural capital was an hour inland by bus along a bumpy road, surrounded by vivid green rice paddies that rose gently to forested slopes beyond. I settled into another guesthouse, this time with simple thatched huts on terraces, and concrete steps and pathways that wound down to a communal bar. An attached bathroom was little more than a lean-to with a flushing toilet, a huge barrel of water and a plastic pail floating on the top. I shaved blind, no mirror, then dipped the pail and dumped sun-warmed water over the top of my head each morning. At night I cleaned my teeth amid a swirl of insects, before stepping back into my room and closing the mosquito net around my bed.

After the dusty frenzy of Kuta Beach, Ubud was peaceful and refined. I walked out on dirt paths through the paddies, past lichen-crusted stone shrines and coconut palms. As far as the trees, the only sound was of trickling water and chirruping crickets; under the forest canopy there were rustles, squawks and flashes of colour. If you stood there long enough, as the insects swarmed above your head, there were louder crashes and cries from deeper in the undergrowth. Never was the Wikipedia phrase "The Bali tiger is extinct" more reassuring. Feeling stronger, I hiked out the few kilometres to Goa Gajah and shuffled through the gaping mouth of a demonic carved face into an ancient cave, where stone idols sat in a recess at the end of a narrow passage.

This was a Bali I could engage with, far away from the surf-and-booze shenanigans of Kuta. Pavilions rose above bougainvillea-clad temple walls in town, with blossom garlands and strips of bright cloth hung around timeworn statues of deities. In the daily market, workshops and craft outlets sold scarves, statues, bags, kites and fans – not a surfboard to be seen. At the Royal Palace, I strolled around the gardens by day and then came back in the evening for a performance of traditional music and dance, the slow ritualised movements accompanied by a lilting *gamelan* orchestra of drums, gongs and xylophones.

Passing the Bumbu Restaurant one day, I saw a notice in the window advertising a cooking class. I'm not a nervous or cautious eater by any means, but since Satay-Gate in Kuta I had taken a circumspect approach to dining out. There were only so many near-death, monkey-strangling experiences a man could have in one trip. But this did seem like a chance to hit refresh. For a few dollars, it was promised, I could learn about authentic Balinese food. Plus, I'd be cooking it myself – no one else to blame.

Next morning at nine, a small group of us met outside the restaurant. Chef, no less, was taking us to the market to shop for the meal.

Chef's English was good, but you had to be concerned about the sort of people he was used to teaching.

In front of market stalls piled high with produce, he plucked a handful of bulbs.

"Very important in Balinese cuisine," he said. "Has anyone seen this before?"

"It's garlic," someone said.

"Oh," said Chef, nonplussed at this unexpected level of expertise. He grabbed something else and brandished it.

"Now these, also very important. Maybe you don't have them in your country, so I'll tell ..."

"Chillies," said a second person.

Crestfallen, Chef's hand hovered over another pile of produce and, to be fair, no one had ever seen his final knobbly root selections before.

"No!", a delighted Chef yelled, "Not ginger! Turmeric! Galangal! Very important." He'd cheered up immensely by the time we got back to the restaurant kitchen.

We donned checked cotton aprons and spent the rest of the morning pounding spice paste in a mortar and pestle, with Chef beetling around making sure we weren't using the wrong chillies.

"Smaller, hotter!", he shouted. It wasn't clear if this was an encouragement or a warning, so mostly we threw in a mix of large and small, green and red. Pieces of ginger and turmeric root went in whole – "No peeling!" – and there was a final scoop of something toe-curlingly pungent that turned out to be fermented shrimp paste. I wasn't sure I'd spread it on toast and have it for breakfast, let's put it like that.

Satay, of course, was on the menu. It was on every menu in Bali, and I was going to have to face up to it again at some point. This seemed like the place.

Chef's special Balinese satay was not the kind you could buy in the street; the one you'd recognise; the one that had done interesting things to my internal organs. *Sate Lilit* was a ceremonial dish that took some amount of preparation – not simple skewered slices of meat but a minced mixture tempered with coconut and sugar which was then wrapped around flat sticks instead. This was satay to be served to a prince, not an Aussie backpacker. It deserved respect.

We blended and mixed, moistened our hands and tried to shape the meat patties around the skewers. Chef did about twenty to each one of ours, laughing with us when bits fell off, which to begin with was every single time – as *lilit* means "to wrap around," I'm not sure our satay shouldn't have had a different name. Whatever the Balinese was for "slap it on any old how." Eventually though we had a platter's worth and Chef fired up the outdoor grill in the restaurant garden.

Grilled over a fire of coconut husks, the satay bubbled and browned. We slid them off the skewers and ate with rice, together with chicken broth, and green beans topped with a spice paste and fresh, grated coconut. It was a happy meal, made by strangers who had bonded over food, and Chef looked proudly on as we reached for seconds and thirds.

I'll admit, I checked for internal gurgling, the tell-tale wince, the strangled cry of the put-upon monkey. But it seemed I was home free.

Finally, in this tale of two satays, the best of times, the season of light, the spring of hope.

A prison break in the South Pacific

A ROCK ADRIFT in the South Pacific, a thousand kilometres east of Australia, six hundred north of New Zealand, and just eight by five across – it's easy to see how you could miss Norfolk Island and the pilot almost does.

"Strong crosswind today folks, we're just going to go round again and have another attempt at landing."

Anyone else unnerved by the idea of having to "have another go at landing"? Call me old-fashioned but I'm a traditionalist when it comes to putting planes on runways. I prefer just one successful go, not several swoop-down and oh-no-back-up-again goes, but maybe that's just me?

The pilot bumps us down eventually on the airstrip at Norfolk Island International Airport – like there's even room for another, domestic, airport – and that's it; paradise awaits on a glorious tropical idyll, at least according to Norfolk Island Tourism. Meanwhile, I'm clutching a copy of *The Fatal Shore* by Robert Hughes, the magisterial account of convict transportation to Australia in the eighteenth century. It's not paradise I'm interested in, rather the forbidding natural prison that was Norfolk Island, "the worst place in the English-speaking world." That phrase – not surprisingly – is absent from the brochures. But maybe I'll find both here – horror and holiday – and, to be fair, the pristine island of sandy beaches and rocky coves doesn't hide its history in the slightest.

Not that there's anywhere to hide anything. Norfolk Island is tiny. I walk from the airport to the main settlement of Burnt Pine, literally just a few metres away from the landing planes, a nondescript, drive-through township with pick-ups and cars parked outside low-rise malls and villas. Shopping centre, post office, bottle shop, a bar at the RSL Club, bistro meals and fish fries at the Bowling Club – so far, so very small-town Australia.

Without the pine trees that rise above the buildings – and that cover large swathes of the coastline and interior – the world might have continued to pass by Norfolk Island. Polynesian settlers landed and lived here many centuries ago, but the island was simply too remote – too far from other trading centres – to sustain a long-term population. It had been uninhabited for hundreds of years when Captain Cook entered its waters in 1774 on his second round-the-world voyage. He named the island after a patron, the Duchess of Norfolk, and noted its characteristic pine trees, growing straight, tall and true – ideal, he thought, for ships' masts. They are shown on the island's flag, and you can still walk amongst fifty-metre-high pines today in the reserve known as the Norfolk Island National Park – again, loving that "national" – which covers much of the northern end of the island. A look-out point surveys the place where Cook landed, with the pines clinging to cliffs that step up and away from the crashing South Pacific.

A few years later, with colonists and convicts struggling to survive at the "First Fleet" settlement of Sydney Cove in Australia, Cook's remote discovery offered some hope. Far off it might be, but Norfolk Island looked like it could sustain a sub-colony and relieve the pressure on New South Wales. Beyond the cliffs, the land seemed rich and fertile, capable of supporting a small township. Flax also grew in abundance, and it was thought that the convicts could establish an industry making canvas, clothes and sails. By 1791, around a thousand people lived on Norfolk Island, three-quarters of them prisoners, the rest soldiers and officers, all transplanted from the Australian mainland.

The British authorities soon discovered what the Polynesians had, centuries before. The land looked gorgeous and plentiful, but it was a constant struggle to carve out any kind of life on the island. The pines proved in the end to be too weak to use as masts, the flax industry failed because no one knew how to prepare the material, and any crops that were planted were ravaged by rats and parrots that scurried and squawked without rest. There were plenty of fish, but they were hard to get at by boat across the booming reefs which could shred a hull in seconds. The one easy source of food was provided by the docile mutton birds, oily and ill-tasting petrels, which flocked in their hundreds of thousands but were slaughtered to extinction within twenty years. By 1814 the island had been abandoned as a lost cause, its buildings dismantled and smallholdings dug up, so that passing ships wouldn't think it worth landing and staking a claim. If the British couldn't make a go of it, even with a free supply of convict labour, they weren't about to relinquish Norfolk Island to another rival nation.

I rent a bike in Burnt Pine and career around on quiet, undulating roads through countryside – away from the coast at least – that looks almost English, as if there's a folk-memory embedded in the landscape by the convicts yearning for home. There are green fields, horse-grazed paddocks, stone walls, rustic wooden fencing, and honesty boxes containing homegrown produce. The wandering cows, it turns out, have right of way on the roads. There are no traffic lights and no house numbers, and if you leave your car unlocked or your bike by the side of the road it will still be there when you get back.

The north is largely tree covered and rises to the island's highest point, Mount Bates, around three hundred metres up. There's not much left of the original rainforest cover, hacked down by setters and pastoralists over the years, but there are still stands of native palms, as well as tree ferns that are claimed to be the tallest on the planet. Any residual Englishness soon evaporates as parrots and other island birds explode from the trees, and insects buzz and chirrup. The noise must have terrified convicts from the London slums who'd never encountered anything larger than a robin.

Heading south instead, I soon pick up the next chapter of the island story by cycling down to the jetty at Kingston. This is where the earliest settlers arrived, put to work erecting buildings that still stand, though they are now in various stages of disrepair. It's preserved as a UNESCO World Heritage Site but, however calm the day and blue the sky, it's a mournful walk between the high walls and monumental gateways of dressed stone.

After being abandoned for ten years to the elements, the buildings were repurposed and added to after 1825, when Norfolk Island was once again used as an escape-proof prison for those deemed to be "the worst of the worst." Double-damned, those brought here for the next thirty years were British and Irish convicts who had already been transported to Australia – often for minor thefts and misdemeanours – and had then offended again. Where else to send them but to the ends of the earth? There was to be no return from Norfolk Island, that "abode of misery."

It's hard – walking on green lawns, overlooking frothing surf, the sun glinting on the Pacific Ocean – to understand the horrors that unfolded here. There are picnic benches under pines near the tower of the old salt mill, and a collapsing fishing boat carcass outside the roofless ruins of the crank-mill. Inside, shackled convicts once turned mill wheels by brute strength in searing heat. Others broke stones from dawn until dusk for the jail, hospital and barracks buildings, whose walls I now trace with my hands as I wander the site. Convicts quarried rocks, cut down trees and made bricks, often clapped in heavy irons, chained at night and surviving on maggot-ridden provisions. Refusal, the breakage of a tool, the wrong word to the wrong person – any minor infringement, at the whim of a soldier or overseer – resulted in floggings so prolonged and brutal that

121

death was judged to be more merciful. Flayed men were locked naked in water-filled, rat-infested cells. Women and girls were not spared, but rather abused, sold and enslaved. Uprisings and mutinies were frequent; none was successful. Floggings, hangings, mutilations and incarcerations followed, year on miserable year.

Norfolk Island still couldn't pay for itself though, stuck at the end of a very long supply line from Blighty via Australia. Finally, in the 1850s, the island was abandoned for a second time, as the remaining convicts were transferred to Tasmania, where similar conditions awaited. Transportation from Britain to the colonies ceased altogether, though let's not get dewy-eyed about it – banging people up in English prisons turned out to be cheaper than sending them halfway across the world, even factoring in the neglect and deaths. Norfolk Island – "Old Hell," a place of ultimate terror – relinquished its horrors and sank back into the stormy embrace of the South Pacific.

Heritage is important, of course, yet there's nothing but shame here, among the ruined buildings that shattered thousands of lives. I don't know if the stones of Kingston speak, but if they do I doubt I'd want to hear them.

I push the bike on down to the harbour. Extraordinarily, two centuries after the convicts first splashed ashore, there's still no proper port on the island. The eighteenth-century Navy ships couldn't get past the encircling reefs and everything had to be unloaded by dinghy. The very first settlement ship to make the journey from Australia in 1790, the *Sirius*, was wrecked on the rocks. Even today, supply ships are emptied by launch, landing to the north at Cascade Bay or here at Kingston's squat concrete jetty. I stick around long enough to watch three guys unload a plastic tray of hefty snapper, which they gut and fillet on the dockside. There are whales offshore they tell me, but I'd need to take a boat out past the pounding surf to have a chance of seeing them.

The only sheltered swimming on the island is east of the jetty, in front of the old settlement buildings, where the reef protects two adjacent lagoons backed by soft, golden sands. Slaughter Bay is a long stretch with rocky outcrops and a name that doesn't do itself any favours, so I push on to the pristine curve of Emily Bay, backed by a line of Norfolk pine trees. It's a beautiful sweep with clear, turquoise water – at the heart of the whole "South Seas Paradise" thing, which for the first time I can just about begin to appreciate, if it wasn't for the whole "South Seas Torture Island" thing. But it's possible, here at least, to dip your toes in the warm water, look out to sea, enjoy a sunset and contemplate better days.

The Norfolk Island story has a final twist, which I begin to unpick in the cemetery, of all places, a little further along the coast. The islanders have been burying people here for over two hundred years – still do, in fact – which makes it a sobering stop, when you consider the realities behind the plain words on the earliest gravestones: executed, killed, died. Few if any expired of natural causes, unless you count fever, illness or accident. Convicts, soldiers, sailors, castaways, whalers, fishermen – each stone tells another story and, because I like cemeteries, I walk among them and touch the headstones, and say hello and sorry.

Once the convicts had gone, Norfolk Island was empty of people for less than a year. In 1856, two hundred people from Pitcairn Island were resettled here, descendants of the HMS *Bounty* mutineers who had outgrown the remote island hide-out that they had chanced upon back in 1790. The evidence is right here, in the ranks of hand-carved gravestones that flow down a contoured green field towards the sand and the waves. The family names of Christian, Quintal, McCoy, Young and others – the original mutineers – loom large in the cemetery and on the island still, where fifty percent of the inhabitants can trace their ancestry back to Pitcairn. In fact, family names are so limited that the Norfolk Island phone directory is searchable by nickname, that being the only reliable way to recognise who's who.

Perhaps this was what was required to breathe permanent life into the island – a new transportation of tight-knit people who were used to eking out a living in one of the most remote places on earth. Norfolk can hardly have seemed intimidating to the isolated souls of Pitcairn, who had already learned to live without help from outside. The new arrivals moved into the abandoned prison buildings, tilled the soil, built boats to fish and didn't fear the lash. They spread out onto farmsteads with their Tahitian wives and partners, and settled and tamed the whole island. The language they spoke with each other was Norfuk, a creole blend of eighteenth-century English and Tahitian, and it's the official joint language today.

I cycle back to Burnt Pine, noticing England and Australia less and Polynesia more. Now the name of my cheery "Aloha Apartment" or the promise of a *hula* dance doesn't seem quite so cheesy. Here's the real spirit of Norfolk Island, distilled not from English and Australian colonisation but from a Pacific brew of welcome and community. It speaks volumes that one of the most popular things to do for tourists is to eat around the island on a "progressive dinner," invited into homes to get to know the locals. On high days and holidays, meat and yams are still cooked over coals in earth ovens, Polynesian style, while other local dishes recall the challenges of older times, like marinated raw fish or dumplings made from unripe green bananas.

Everything has changed in two hundred years and yet not everything has. Although a territory of Australia, Norfolk Island was self-governing until 2015 when its autonomy was removed. It now sits uneasily offshore, sharing New South Wales' laws and regulations, the inhabitants liable for the first time to income tax, which has gone down about as well as you might imagine. Despite the air link, the island remains tangibly remote, its facilities – schools, hospitals, infrastructure – underfunded, with tourism its best and only hope for the future. Burnt Pine might not be much – looking around, this is rural Australian life rather than a bustling capital – but it's all there is.

Sustainability – that's what it's always come down to on Norfolk Island. A couple of thousand people living on a speck of South Pacific rock, at the end of a supply line, with nowhere else to go, trying to make the best of things.

A road trip in Ghana

I WAS BORN in Ghana, West Africa. I sometimes think it's the single most noteworthy thing that's ever happened to me.

Place of birth: Takoradi, Ghana. It's on my birth certificate, passport, driving licence and CV, so it comes up as a subject more often than you'd think. I even have an unofficial Ghanaian name – Yaw, pronounced "Yow" – which, as is traditional in some African cultures, reflects the day of the week on which I was born, Thursday.

Weather-wise, I'm a reluctant Englishman, preferring warmer seasons and countries which, I like to think, has something to do with my tropical birthplace. I go running in a canary-yellow Ghanaian football shirt – this is a good idea because the paramedics will be able to pick me out – and I have some Ghanaian highlife and hip-hop CDs that I inflict on guests, because I was born in Ghana you know. Look, it's my thing. I never once had a trial for a professional football team or was in the same college class as the Prime Minister. I never released a single on a minor record label that got to number eighty-three in the Belgian charts, but I was born in what sounds like an exotic place.

When it does come up as a subject, people then often say, "Really? That's interesting. What's it like? What do you miss about Ghana?" Because it's unusual for someone like me – a white, middle-aged, ostensibly Yorkshire person called Julian – to come from West Africa. I live in a small English market town. No one knows I have a secret day-name. I'm not the obvious candidate.

The question is my chance to shine. This should be the point at which anecdotes flow.

"He was a git then and he's a git now," I'd say of the Prime Minister. Or "Just five more sales and we'd have been in the Walloon Top Eighty."

But I have nothing. I've built myself up as someone with a backstory that sounds fascinating, and which should explain all sorts of things about me. Unfortunately, I have nowhere to go with it. Each time, I listen to myself say, "Ah, well, the thing is, I left when I was ten months old. I don't have any memories of Ghana at all I'm afraid."

Cue dinner-party silence, broken only by someone turning to another guest and saying "Eighty-three, really? Will I have heard it? Give us the chorus, go on!"

So although it's true, I was born in West Africa, it turns out it's not as interesting as I think it is. But I have a cunning plan.

When I said I left for England when I was just under a year old, I didn't mean that I did this whole Africa business on my own, before I could even walk or talk. That would have been an anecdote worth telling. Instead, I had parents, Jean and Ken, one of whom gave birth to me in Takoradi General Hospital and the other of whom carried me back to their colonial bungalow in a Moses basket. No memory of this, obviously, and no chance to make any memories either, since ten months later we were all on a boat to Liverpool, leaving Baby Me with perhaps just the residual, unconscious feeling that the warm, surrounding, tropical stuff had all gone and in its place was this wet, cold English stuff that I really didn't like one bit.

The parents, though, they had memories of Ghana. I'd heard them all growing up, it's just that they weren't about me, except in the incidental, baby-in-the-corner sort of way. What with the sailing regattas and social clubs, weekly dances and beach trips, I largely got the impression that I must have bottle-fed myself and sorted out my own peek-a-boo sessions while my parents were busy being young and carefree.

I was in my mid-forties by now, which made them – quick calculation – seventy-something. They had never been back since leaving in 1963 and, if I could only persuade them to travel to Ghana with me, I could piggy-back on their collective memory and even come up with some African experiences of my own. I'd have Ghanaian things to talk about at parties.

They could probably cope with the rigours of the trip. My folks were not obviously senile, and at least no more eye-rollingly deranged than any other parent. All I needed to do was surreptitiously check they were fit enough to make the trip, ensure the insurance covered old-people incidents, bring the subject round to holidays, dismiss the idea of a cruise, introduce the good old days and – oh right, they were up for it quicker than you could say "Belgian chart-topper." Dad even went to look for his old safari suit.

We arrived in Accra where, on the advice of the guidebook, we acquired a driver for a three-week trip around my parents' old haunts. This took some persuasion, because at first Dad was very keen on doing the driving himself. I was familiar with the stories. How in the early Sixties he and my mother had travelled overland on jaunts in an Austin A40 loaded with spare fuel cans, emergency supplies and a baby basket. If there was ever any doubt about my role in their adventures it was dispelled by the account of the two-hundred-kilometre drive east to neighbouring Togo. Newly independent, like Ghana, but as a former French protectorate, Togo was a francophone country where imported wine was cheap to buy.

"We loaded up a crate," said Dad, "and shoved it in the back, with you on top in the basket." The Togolese and Ghanaian border authorities were not about to disturb a sleeping baby, so my parents got their contraband wine back into the country without paying any duty.

"There were no seatbelts in the car of course," said Dad, "so you bounced around quite a bit on the rough roads, but not to worry" – and you'll like this bit – "*the wine was fine.*"

So yes, bottom line – I was basically used as an infant smuggler and exposed to physical danger by two bootlegger teachers who fancied themselves as Bonnie and Clyde. I could probably still have had them both arrested.

Even Dad was forced to accept that his driving experience in Ghana – forty years previously, when the country had about eight cars – was not going to cut it. Just the taxi ride from the airport to the hotel gave a flavour of the speed, obduracy and whole-road approach of the local drivers. It was like one giant video game being played out in real time. Whenever we stopped at a traffic light or road junction, vendors appeared at the windows and while the taxi driver did his best – "Please, don't open the ... oh" – we arrived at the hotel with several bead necklaces, a road map of Ghana and some carved wooden elephants.

Obviously, this was never going to work. Our hotel recommended Patrick instead, who had a business card to establish his driving credentials – just one as it happened, because he asked for it back at the end of the trip.

At first Patrick seemed nonplussed that we didn't want to go anywhere touristy, well known or attractive, but instead wanted driving to the industrial port town of Takoradi, where my parents had inexplicably chosen to live. His confusion was understandable – the *Rough Guide to West Africa*, for example, says of Takoradi, "By no stretch of the imagination is it a scenic coastal stop ... it has few redeeming features." The *Bradt Ghana Travel Guide* says, "It seldom inspires affection in travellers." I say, way to go Mum and Dad, top choice.

But once he'd accepted the inevitable – and that Dad was going to sit up front next to him for three weeks and tell him what the roads used to be like twenty years before he was born – Patrick rose magnificently to the challenge.

He piled us and our bags into his thirty-year-old Nissan Patrol, complete with cracked windscreen and compromised air-con, and drove us back into Mum and Dad's past. There was a bit of "Sir" and "Madam" business early on, and he had to be prevented from leaping out at every stop to open the doors for us, but Patrick soon established that Ken and Jean really weren't here on holiday. They had come to track down their former lives and show their baby boy what he had missed. Their baby *Ghanaian* boy, no less – I got a high-five and a complicated fist-bump for that piece of information – meaning that Patrick bought wholeheartedly into the expedition from the off.

It's a couple of hundred kilometres along the coastal route to Takoradi, first trailing out through the extended and congested suburbs of Accra. The roads were lined with stalls, shops and workshops, from simple upturned boxes piled carefully with little pyramids of pawpaws, through metal frames shaded with straw, tin or cloth, to large, open lockups with shelves and a counter. You could buy pretty much anything at any point – wooden furniture being made on the spot, coffins, sandals, hubcaps, mobile phones, eggs, T-shirts and wicker brooms. Ghanaian shop names, by the way, are just the best. Sweet Jesus Fashion Centre; Lady Diana Trading Enterprises; Only Jesus Can Do Mobile Phone Repairs; The Blood of Jesus Fast Foods; and God is Above All Enterprises – the latter, finest purveyors of metalwork and fencing, if that wasn't clear.

Patrick was no mere driver. From the first day onwards, he was pretty much in charge of operations, steering us through markets, changing money and warding off potential guides and hustlers. We were definitely "his" charges, he'd snagged us, and you with the wooden carvings and ingratiating manner can back right off.

He also had a roster of cafés and restaurants in every town – presumably with a kickback for delivering us there, and why not? – where Mum and Dad would share a sandwich and wilt in the midday heat. At their most salubrious, these were straight-up restaurants with air-conditioning. At their most authentic, they were "chop bars" – basic roadside cafés, with a tarp hung over plastic tables, called things like Stomach Care Garden or Top Food Emporium. As an honorary Ghanaian I was expected to join Patrick in a daily mound of chicken *jollof* rice, which is a simmered tomato rice dish flavoured, if that's the word, with bad-boy chillies that would fuel a Mars mission. A couple of mouthfuls in and you'd think, this isn't so bad; five minutes later the droplets falling from your eyes would be melting the plastic tablecloth. Incidentally, saying "But I thought this was a Nigerian dish" is a good way to have your birthplace, heritage and traditional day-name questioned by the driver, chef and anyone else in the café at the time.

There was one other stop before Takoradi, at Cape Coast, former British colonial capital of the Gold Coast and site of one of Ghana's infamous slaving castles. On a sober guided tour we saw the dungeons where captives were held before being herded through "the door of no return" onto the slave ships. We listened to the horrifying statistics – twelve million people enslaved, eighty percent of whom died before they ever reached their destination. And I was unexpectedly moved by the guide's thoughtful, final speech about the need for the Ghanaian diaspora to come back here at least once in their life ("before the Lord calls them") to understand their roots. Despite my birthplace, I was not and could never really be Ghanaian; but that was the first time I felt the slightest genuine tug of a connection to a country I'd never known.

In Takoradi that slight tug turned into something more concrete, as between them Mum, Dad and Patrick left no stone unturned in their pursuit of 1960s' Ghana. Every now and again, when things looked sticky, I was called upon to utter the magic incantation – "I was born here, my name is Yaw." This literally opened doors in places as diverse as the Government Tourist Office, the Secondary Technical School and Takoradi Polytechnic where Dad once taught and, finally, Takoradi General Hospital, scene of my first and greatest appearance.

I've got a photograph of Mum and I sitting on a bed in what used to be the old maternity ward, forty-five years on, mother and son, hand in hand. It's very sweet.

Actually, I have two photos, because it turned out that the first hospital we blagged our way into was not the one in which I was born.

"I didn't think I recognised it," said Mum, after diligent questioning of the staff had revealed that we were in the wrong part of town, in the wrong hospital, sitting in a ward that had never delivered babies, Ghanaian, English or otherwise. By this time, we had already shaken hands with the Medical Director, been accompanied down corridors by beaming security guards and asked several nurses to stop looking after sick and feeble patients so that they could take photographs for us.

"And you were going to mention this, when?"

"Well, I didn't like to say. You seemed so happy to be here dear."

This is why, as a rule, you don't go on holiday with parents.

Anyway, the second photo is definitely in the right hospital, Mum said she was sure this time. She also said that I would dine out on the story for years. Oh no mother, small, select dinner parties are not nearly of the scale required to allow others to appreciate what I had to put up with. I'm putting it in a book.

After a few days in Takoradi, I began to see something else in my parents besides benign incompetence. They had been young and happy here in a newly independent Ghana. They had a life before me and then, briefly, with me, where they worked and socialised, met friends, shopped and went on holiday. Like normal people; like you and I; not like, you know, parents.

We even managed to track down the two houses they had lived in, one now derelict and tumbledown, the other, a bungalow in a sad state of repair but apparently still occupied. I'd have left it at that and snapped a photo from the road but Mum, dander up, hospital fiasco forgotten, was having none of it.

"They won't mind. Anyway, it's our house."

"Well, technically … "

But she had already badgered Dad to knock on the door, determined there was no one home, and then corralled us all around the back into the garden, where she took another photograph of me sitting on the porch where she used to stand my baby basket in the shade.

"And you're sure this is the right house, Mum?"

"Well of course I am," she said, in a bold tone for a woman who had broken at least half a dozen by-laws and health and safety regulations already that day.

Dad, too, was different in a way that I couldn't put my finger on at first. And then, as I watched him negotiate the encounters with students and teachers in his old schools, chat to Patrick about the relative fuel economy of a Nissan Patrol versus, say, an Austin A40, and haggle cheerfully with market traders, it struck me. He was still Dad ("Well, they've let that lathe go, it wants a drop of WD40") but he was more at ease than I'd ever seen him. He fitted in here. He seemed to belong. Yes, in a sort of semi-colonial way – he'd had the luxury of being able to come and go, see the world and enrich his life. But he didn't talk down to anyone and he was genuinely interested in people. He might have been embarrassing to his blinkered, fretful son, but *he* wasn't embarrassed. He was confident, friendly and approachable. I could see why he'd been good at his job and why he'd spent his career travelling the world in technical education, doing something he believed in.

Who knew? Parents are people too.

With the Takoradi memorial visit now concluded, we were free to return to Accra, though – entirely predictably, if you knew my Dad – via a three-hundred-kilometre inland detour to the city of Kumasi. I checked this wasn't one of his fuel- or time-efficiency wheezes, because with him you never knew.

"It might be hundreds of kilometres longer, but it does shave a minute off the travel time" – that would be an entirely normal thing for him to say. At home, he'd set off on the two-hour drive to my house and arrive about five hours later, having plotted a meandering route through every small town within a radius of a hundred miles "because it avoids the motorway," like that was a good thing.

Kumasi, though, turned out to be a genuine target for my parents, because they wanted to recreate part of their greatest overland journey while living in Ghana, the four-day expedition they had made to Paga in the extreme north. That's an undertaking even today. Back then, it required a vehicle-full of tinned food, paraffin, pressure stove, cooking utensils, car tools, spare parts, tow rope, first-aid kit and mosquito repellent. The roads were mostly red laterite and incredibly dusty, and rivers often had to be crossed by rudimentary ferries rather than bridges; vast areas were still marked on the map as "uninhabited." Even so, Mum and Dad had reached Kumasi on the first day and remembered it fondly and, to be fair, Ghana's second city, the old royal capital of the Ashanti state, seemed like a fine place to spend some time.

Unfortunately, Kumasi was not prepared for a second visit from Mum.

"I don't recognise any of it," she complained, for about the fortieth time, as if it was somehow Kumasi's fault for developing over the last four decades since she had bounced in driving an overloaded Austin A40. She was particularly perplexed by the forest of TV aerials, phone masts and antennae which, you'll be surprised to learn, were not a feature of 1960s' Ghana, and she virtually had a meltdown every time she saw someone using a mobile phone.

"Why do they need phones? What do they need to talk about? We used to manage perfectly well without one."

I know. Believe me, I know.

By general agreement, the one place that hadn't changed much in forty years was the market. Our guesthouse insisted on providing a guide, which seemed entirely redundant until we got there and discovered that Kejeta market is the largest in West Africa and occupies most of the city centre. It's probably fairer to say that Kumasi is in the market, rather than the market being in Kumasi. We took a deep breath and plunged in behind the guide, Mum muttering about phones, Dad inspecting random stalls with the air of a man hoping to happen upon a secondhand three-amp fuse "because it'll come in handy."

If you took your eye off the guide for even a second, you were lost. In a crush of humanity, between wooden stalls with tin roofs in narrow alleys, the people came in waves, carrying bags, pushing carts, bearing packs on their backs, and balancing baskets, buckets and bales on their heads. Step aside to allow someone past and you couldn't get back into the slow, purposeful flow; stand still and you'd suddenly find yourself swept a few metres back and sideways, waving frantically at an elderly woman saying "Well I don't recognise that stall" and a man who had just inadvertently bought a piece of plastic tubing.

The market was split into distinct areas – neighbourhoods, really – devoted to entire goods and trades, from butchers to jewellers, cloth-sellers to pottery-makers. That it was like no market I'd ever been to before was immediately apparent, as we were led past fly-ridden hunks of freshly hacked antelope, piles of pigs' trotters, buckets of intestines and trays of giant, stripy land snails, each the size of a clenched fist. One man pushed past carrying a severed cow's head on each shoulder, so that was going to be a treat for someone – date night, presumably. There were tomatoes, chillies, onions and plantains being sold from trays by women squatting on the ground in the shade, but once you've seen a man with a head of cattle on either side of his own head, it's going to take a shockingly deformed vegetable to grab your attention.

At one point we spent a good five minutes circling tables filled with contorted lengths of dried and smoked fish before emerging into what was clearly the Peanut Butter Zone, where volcano-shaped mounds of glistening brown sludge oozed in the wet heat of the day. This was for making the staple Ghanaian dish of groundnut stew, a fiery peanut and chicken curry that can singlehandedly double your body-mass-index and which I'd already been talked into by Patrick more than once as a light and refreshing lunchtime snack.

Sidling down another alley, Dad's eyes lit up at the sight of men gluing soles to old car tyres, cutting them out and fixing straps, to sell on as sandals. Others were delving into piles of metal junk and fashioning scraps into rudimentary tools, knives and even musical instruments. Bits of wood were being cut and sawed into useful lengths; electrical wire was being stripped from machinery and rolled around bobbins or used to connect other things together.

This extreme recycling in action was basically Dad's Womble-like garage on an industrial scale, where nothing he had ever owned was thrown away or wasted because "You never know when you might need it."

Well, I can tell you when I didn't need it. After he died, when I had to make approximately a hundred journeys in the car to the municipal tip with labelled coffee jars of "screws, assorted" and "carpet tacks, used," miles of electrical cabling, dozens of half-empty tins of paint, every plastic takeaway container ever delivered to the house, the entire fitted kitchen-before-last, two defunct roller-blade lawnmowers (using one of which, he had actually severed his big toe, so you'd have thought he'd have wanted to get rid of that), scores of sockets and plugs dating back to the 1970s, machine oils of dubious provenance, two children's bikes (I was fifty-three) and an unrivalled collection of splintered door frames.

Back in Kumasi, as he roamed the alley with a gleam in his eye, I could see Dad calculating wildly the prospect of getting some of these recycled items – any of them – on the plane home. I could also hear a lone voice shouting "Ken, come away, you don't need it," so that was his goose cooked.

We climbed up a narrow staircase and shuffled along a rickety verandah, from where there was a view of tin roofs, straw hats, head-coverings and bobbing baskets as far as the eye could see. Precariously balanced prefabs and shacks crowded both sides of the alleys below. The market was simply vast, with other sections out of sight beyond the low rise in the land ahead. Further north still was the district known as Magazine, which sold only wrecked vehicles, engines and spare parts – we drove through later on the way home, picking our way around vehicles being disembowelled by guys with wrenches and tyre irons. And to reinforce the point that this was more than just a market, we followed the noise of a mechanical chattering from a nearby terrace, which revealed itself to be a cramped sweatshop – scores of men and women at battered, rusty sewing machines turning out school uniforms, shirts and dresses at a phenomenal pace.

The entire market was a remarkable enterprise. This wasn't just shopping, this was life –hard, hot, messy, smelly, noisy and entirely normal. People did come here to buy things every day, but they also came to deliver, fetch, carry, work, eat, drink and socialise, and many of them never left because they lived here too.

In the end, I left Mum and Dad in a chop bar, reclining on plastic seats and sipping lukewarm Cokes, while Patrick took over from the guide and steered me along the disused railway line that cut through part of the market. Like men the world over, during our trip we'd bonded over football and music, and Patrick was on a mission to make me more Ghanaian before I went home.

We walked between the dusty tracks, past stalls selling monkey skulls, desiccated chameleons, skins, pelts and dried plants – fetishes for religious rituals – and it was a mark of this extraordinary day that, by now, this barely raised an eyebrow. Instead, we had our eyes on Ghanaian football magazines and music CDs, and for a few bucks I secured the basis of much more satisfying conversations when the matter of my birthplace came up.

I no longer envied the Belgian chart-nudgers. I had stories, I had evidence, I was ready to go.

"You were born in Ghana, really? That's interesting. What's it like?"

Funny you should ask.

A summer to remember in Scotland

"HOW COME YOU never mention me in any of your travel stories?" says Elaine.

I'm tempted to say that I just have, and write "The End", but I have a feeling that won't go down well.

She has a point. Mostly, I write in the first person. I go to places and report back. There is the occasional "we" in my stories and adventures, and sometimes that other person is Elaine and sometimes it isn't. But I hardly ever name names and, Elaine is right, she is never mentioned. Though we are up to three times now in the first hundred words, so I'm trying my best here.

Actually, what she really means is, "Look buster, how come you didn't mention me, when I was there with you on that trip?"

At least it sounds like "buster". Elaine is and can speak Irish, and the only Irish word I know is *sasanach*, which if you're English can be considered more or less derogatory depending on context. If an Irish person calls you a *sasanach*, you need to check if they are smiling at you or chasing you with a pointed stick.

What she's driving at is my tendency to pretend that I was on my own in a place when I wasn't.

She'll peer over my shoulder as I'm writing sometimes and say, "That's very funny, only wasn't that actually my joke?"

Or she'll say, "Why don't you put me in that bit? After all, I drove you there."

It's true, that this is how I present most of my travels – as if I was there on my own. And quite often I was. For almost all my guidebook days for Rough Guides I travelled solo because, let's face it, no one wanted to come to the timber-filled towns of central Sweden for two months to watch me copy down restaurant menus and inspect backpacker hostels.

But I've also spent thirty-odd years travelling with other people – on press trips, weekends away, city breaks, journeys, excursions and even good old holidays. Yet I've written many of these trips up as if I went on my own – even, dare I say, some of the stories in this book.

It isn't, I hope, an ego thing. It's not about advertising my importance. The destinations – the places I go – all get on fine without me, I'm sure.

But it is a conscious decision and, without sounding too pretentious, it's about style. I've never been a "my companion and I" kind of travel writer, skimming the surface of a destination. I think my job is to do a bit more than just describe and inform. I enjoy visiting places that provoke thoughts and feelings, and I like to share those. Sense of place is important to me; I want to transmit the kind of details that really help you understand what a place looks, feels and smells like. And while I have lots of my own experiences to draw upon, I also spend quite a lot of time eavesdropping, listening in, overhearing, or watching from afar and then writing down the good bits.

Presenting it all as a single, personal experience helps crystallise the things that I have understood about a destination. I like to think that my writing has a strength and a flow that derives from this first-person telling – without getting sidetracked by mentions of friends, companions and strangers, whose names and presence you then have to register. With my writing, on the whole you don't have to ask yourself who this Dave is, who has just made a most excellent joke about Swedish timber production. I just nick Dave's joke and use it to embellish my own account, because I think it will make for a better read.

None of this butters any parsnips with Elaine, who fixes me with the sort of look she usually reserves for English people who insist – despite her repeated corrections – that she comes from "Southern Ireland." The sort of look you would receive if you pointed out that, technically, Ireland forms part of what's known as the "British Isles," and don't give me that look, I didn't come up with the designation, talk to the geographers.

She is not a Dave, Elaine points out. She is my beloved. And it's about time she got some credit.

So because I know what's good for me – i.e. Elaine – I'm sharing the story of a trip we made together that, in normal circumstances, I might be tempted to pass off as my own singular experience. A story that comes with Added Elaine and that will be all the better for it.

"You pick a place," says Elaine, "you're the travel writer and I really don't mind."

We have been seeing each other for a few months. Summer's coming up. A first holiday together has been mentioned.

To be fair to Elaine, knowing that I'm a travel writer, she could have certain reasonable expectations. She knows that I have written books about Sicily, Spain and Portugal, for example. She's seen the map, she knows how far south they are. We have talked about sitting in cafés, overlooking harbours, eating seafood and drinking chilled wine. We've looked forward to long, lazy strolls in Mediterranean towns and nightcaps under palm trees.

"Ullapool," I say.

"Right," she says.

"It's in Scotland. Quite a long way up in Scotland."

"Right," she says again. "Does it have summer?"

"Does it have summer?", I say. "You bet it has summer. It has an oceanic climate and an average of 1,105 sunshine hours per year."

"Have you been looking at the internet?", says Elaine.

I have. Although it sounds impressive, eleven hundred hours of sunshine a year actually isn't very much. I have also omitted the part about Ullapool being cloudier than any other place in Europe. That seems to me to be on a need-to-know basis. If you draw a horizontal line on a map, Ullapool is at about the same latitude as Newfoundland, Norway and Estonia, none of which are known for their balmy summers. I decide not to mention that either.

"And why are we going to Ullapool?", says Elaine.

I'm on firmer ground here. Because it sounds really cool. Because it's on a deep loch surrounded by gnarled mountains and looks a little bit like Norway transplanted to Scotland. Because it's further north than Moscow and because Russian fishing vessels used to pitch up and drink the local pubs dry, just like in *Local Hero*. Because neither of us has ever been and getting there will be an adventure.

Although I don't know her very well yet, I do know that if Elaine says she really doesn't mind something, then she doesn't. She's positive and enthusiastic about everything. She sees the best in everyone and every situation. Elaine will not be counting the hours of sunshine and examining the cloud layer, and then bringing up the damning facts later in a general discussion about the shortcomings of my holiday choice. If I say Ullapool will be cool, she's happy to take my word for it and throw herself into the adventure. This wholesome approach to life is one of the innumerable reasons that, many years later, she is still my beloved and getting a whole story to herself.

We drive up to Ullapool from northern England, which turns out to be quite the undertaking, involving driving half the length of the entire UK. That will teach me for looking at the Google map and thinking it looked about six inches away. It takes three hours just to cross the border, after which there is still a lot of Scotland to go. The scenery becomes increasingly dramatic as we skirt the Cairngorms en route to Inverness, barrelling along the A9, the longest road in Scotland. It's wild, big-sky country, on a route that sweeps over passes and down through broad valleys, past isolated dwellings and hamlets.

By now the road signs are in Gaelic as well as English, which is close enough to Irish at times for Elaine to offer a running commentary on the presumed attractions of the places we pass.

"Let's see, 'the bright harbour of the gentle fairy' is in fact … wait for it, let me look, oh a tweed factory outlet."

The weather is entirely as predicted, which is to say cloudy. For the last hour of the drive – through bleak moorland and past bare hills and grey-tinted lochs – it gets progressively darker, until the final run along the eastern shore of Loch Broom when the weather basically goes, sod it, and slings sheets of heavy rain against the windscreen. We follow the SatNav to the holiday cottage we've rented, high above the loch, and traipse around after the owner through damp-smelling room after damp-smelling room as she points out the wood-burning stove and the storage radiators for "if it gets a wee bit chilly in the evenings."

If. Wee bit.

You can see your breath in the air outside. Rain is lashing against a window that should, in theory, offer an uninterrupted view over the glories of Ullapool but instead offers an unrivalled view of rain. In the chilliness stakes, the house is whatever the opposite of a "wee bit" is. It's late afternoon in August. This is our summer holiday.

"Does it ever stop raining?", I ask.

"I don't know," says the woman, "I'm only fifty-five."

We both think we're joking, but it's difficult to tell.

Elaine and I wait until we hear her car disappear down the drive and then switch on every radiator we can find. We locate the wood store and light the log-burner and make a pinkie-promise that it is never to go out, not on our watch, no sirree. We leaf through the binder of information about the house, where there are humorous injunctions against using the heating in summer unless you want to be liable for a twenty-five-pound surcharge. We laugh – laugh I tell you! – in the face of such impertinence, safe in the knowledge that we've spent twenty-five quid in the last hour already and there's plenty more where that came from. Over the next week, our proudest achievement is that we kept that sucker burning twenty-four-seven, until we could bask in the lounge in T-shirts and sip the best – all right, only – cheeky little rosé that Ullapool's Tesco could provide.

Although I don't know her very well yet, I am comforted by the fact that Elaine would rather be warm than cold. She doesn't ask why I have switched the oven on and propped its door open, and I have to say I like that in a person.

Because it's our first night and it's freezing, we pile log upon log for later and call a taxi to take us the short distance into town for dinner. Because, drinking. And rain.

We get a very chatty taxi driver who fulfils all the possible impenetrable-accent clichés you could want by being virtually impossible to understand while sat in the back seat of a Skoda Octavia. As she turfs us out in a backstreet in Ullapool, she hands us a card that says "Pam's Taxis" and says, "Gi' us a call, when you want a toksi, ask for Pom."

I have never heard anyone do that to vowels before. Pom, needless to say, is our go-to gal for toksis for the rest of the week.

Dinner is in The Ceilidh Place, which is recommended far and wide but is on the wee bit chilly side too. I'd say that I'm overly sensitive – born in Africa, fan of the Med, constitutionally averse to cold weather – except that Elaine is from County Wicklow where, as far as anyone knows, it has never stopped raining. And she thinks they should switch their heating up too, so we finish dinner quickly and walk around the harbour to The Ferry Boat Inn for a nightcap before summoning Pom.

To me, a nightcap is another glass of red wine and an espresso if they have one. I don't expect to sleep, don't worry. But the bar in the Ferry Boat Inn prides itself on its single malt whiskies and, if you like that sort of thing, you're in for a treat. The Scots do love whisky, it's a fact. They bang on about the distilleries, the peat and the smoky taste, all night if you let them. The Ferry Boat Inn has about a thousand different varieties on little shelves and a very keen barman who can tell you at which remote waterfall they collected the water and what side of the valley the peat was dug.

"Will you have a wee dram of whisky?", he says. "Our single malts are very special. You should have one. Here, let me recommend one for you."

He has no idea.

What you have to understand about an Irishwoman of certain opinion is that she has endured eight hundred years of being told what to do by non-Irish people, mostly English it's true, but anyone in the UK basically has to watch their step.

"Do you have a Jameson's?", says Elaine. She pronounces it "Jemmeson's", like it should be pronounced and not like the way English or Scottish people say it.

"I don't think I'm familiar with that name," says the barman boldly, for he has no idea.

"Well, I don't really like Scottish whisky," says Elaine. "So I'd prefer a Jameson's, the Irish whiskey, I'll have one of those."

He looks aghast – "not liking" Scottish whisky has clearly never occurred to him as a concept. Also, he has no idea he's just been schooled in the use of the extra and correct Irish 'e' in the word "whiskey."

Because I don't know her very well yet, this is a revelation to me. I would have drunk the Scottish whisky, just to be polite. I'm English, and if there's one thing an English person is more afraid of than making a fuss in public it's upsetting a Scottish person. It usually ends badly on a battlefield somewhere.

But Elaine is proudly Irish and, as she has pointed out, she doesn't like the peaty, smoky Scottish stuff, however much you bang on about it. She wants and gets a proper whiskey by simply asking for it, and I can see that this confidence is a useful skill to have. I make a note to stick closely to her, on the basis that if I find myself being too English for my own good, I can always get an Irishwoman of certain opinion to do my asking for me.

The next day it's overcast and drizzling, which is a distinct improvement in the summer weather, so we take the chance to look around Ullapool between showers.

It's only small – a couple of thousand people all told – with a grid of white-painted houses spreading across a small promontory sticking out into the loch. It wouldn't be exactly right to call the town attractive, but that's not exactly fair either. It's a working port, with all that that entails, and it doesn't have anything to prove to the likes of us. But the location is stunning, on a narrow fjord hemmed in by mountains that are the very definition of sullen and brooding on a day like today. A Viking called Ulla probably settled down here some time back in the ninth century – I dare say the terrible weather reminded him of home – and for hundreds of years afterwards Ullapool comprised just a few crofts and farms clinging tenaciously to both sides of Loch Broom, making the sort of living that never bothered anyone.

The modern town dates back around two hundred and fifty years, to when herring started to be landed here in huge numbers. The British Fisheries Society planned for grand things and laid out orderly streets, public buildings and a large harbour with curing sheds and warehouses. What they hadn't bargained for was the disappearance of the herring shoals from the whole of the west coast, which ruined the new town within twenty years. It wasn't until the 1970s that Ullapool was a successful fishing port once again, this time attracting Russian factory ships.

That era has gone too now, leaving tourism as the mainstay, though life still revolves around the deep-water harbour. While we watch, ferries come and go to Stornaway in the Outer Hebrides, and tons of other smaller boats flit about in the mid-distance, doubtless doing complicated things with fish and nets. I'm always rather in awe of people who make a living from the sea. Fair play to them. On any given day, I can think of many, many things that I would rather do than ride the swell in a freezing sea with chaps in yellow oils manhandling a great deal of ice and fish.

We make a discovery, which is that there is a little man in a car park with a fresh fish stall. He sells us a slab of hake off a boat and half a dozen enormous scallops, which he claims have been hand-gathered by a man in a diving suit. Which is entirely the sort of thing I might tell two tourists if I was trying to get them to part with their money. To give him his due, the fish and shellfish are amazing – beautifully firm, fresh and sweet – and a trip to the fish stall becomes a regular occurrence. By the end of the week we are flash-frying scallops in butter for breakfast, just because we can, and although I don't know Elaine very well yet, it seems to me that I could spend more of my days with someone who will gladly eat hand-dived scallops for breakfast.

Over the next few days we venture further out, driving on wild and winding roads to places with extraordinarily alluring names – Achiltibuie ('field of the yellow-haired boy'), Inchnadamph ('meadow of the stags') and SasanachEejit ('missed turn by the English driver'), although I think Elaine is making one of those up. When the clouds clear, we look out from the fractured coastline to the uninhabited Summer Isles and idly wonder how much an island costs these days. By the lonely, waterside ruins of Ardvreck Castle on Loch Assynt, we brush through wet heather to stand in the shelter of five-hundred-year-old stones and idly wonder how much a castle costs these days. Idle wondering is very much the pastime *du jour* on these drives, on account of the rolling mist and the ever-present sound of the pattering rain.

"Is this still my summer holiday?", says Elaine, pointedly emphasizing the word "summer." I assure her it is and switch the heating up in the car.

At Lochinver, an hour's drive from Ullapool, we see a sign saying "Pie Shop", which is a very cheering thing to spot on a Scottish summer holiday. We stock up in the Lochinver Larder and then drive further north around the coast on a precarious road to Achmelvich and Clachtoll. Even in the rain, we can see that these deserted beaches are something special. Grassy mounds and black rocks tumble down to perfect arcs of white sand, and despite the half-light of a rain-soaked August the water has a hint of turquoise in it. We dare each other to stand barefoot in the freezing surf and then, before I know it, Elaine has gone one further. She strips down to a concealed bathing suit, strides in and dips her shoulders under, swimming in water that is turning my feet blue. I resist every entreaty and threat because I'm laughably and reservedly English – no it's freezing, don't be daft, what if someone sees us – and not outgoing and Irish – ah sure it's grand, you big eejit.

We sit under blankets in collapsible camping chairs that we have wrestled across the dunes, and eat pies and drink thermos-flask tea under an umbrella that is really only big enough for one. We watch dark clouds roil the sky and warm our fingers on hot plastic cups.

"Is this still my summer holiday?", says Elaine. I assure her that it is and wipe drops of rain from her cheek.

Even now, years later, I can't guarantee that I can tell you what colour Elaine's eyes are, how many cousins she's got or what her confirmation name is. She'll have a favourite colour, I'm sure, but I couldn't tell you what it is. I'm only a man after all.

But I remember every second of Ullapool in all its glorious, rain-spattered, log-fire-burning, breath-chilling, toksi-taking clarity. And I can recall the point at which I stopped not knowing Elaine very well and started thinking about the future. About travelling together, finding our place in the world and growing old in each other's company. About making each other better by being together, sitting hand in hand on remote white-sand beaches, and hoping for the sun but never minding the rain.

A long and lazy lunch in Ibiza

LET'S NOT WORRY too much about why we were in Ibiza.

Not really our kind of place, we'd always thought, until it turned into potentially our kind of place by virtue of the never-ending British winter, followed by a damp, dismal spring and the siren lure of a bargain airfare.

The plane descended over a twinkling blue ocean, sandy bays and palm trees, which was a good start. Even so, still not really our kind of place, we thought, as we exited the airport past billboards for clubs featuring DJs called things like XXXMixx and not Disco Dave – DJs who played "beats" and "bangers" and not proper music like "Dancing Queen". Clubs that didn't open – open, I tell you – their doors until midnight, or two hours after bedtime as it's more usually known. But then it turned out that none of the clubs opened at all before the season started again in May, and Ibiza suddenly moved up a notch or two in our reckoning. It was in Spain after all – or at least part *of* Spain – and Spain was definitely our kind of place. Spain, we liked.

On the way into Ibiza Town in the taxi it was clear that the pool-and-villa-party club gates were firmly locked, last year's posters unfurling from the walls. The beaches were deserted and the houses still shuttered against the spring squalls. We checked into an empty apartment complex, where the swimming pool was drained of water and the lounge chairs stacked against a wall that needed a fresh coat of paint.

Yet the temperature held at a steady twenty degrees Celsius, even in March. The trees were full of oranges, with white blossom gathered in small kerbside drifts. Hidden courtyards opened up off white-painted streets, overlooked by balconies filled with flowering tubs. Sturdy castle ramparts marched across piercingly blue skies, while a gentle ocean breeze ruffled the blazing gorse bushes and wild oregano that carpeted the surrounding slopes.

We tramped the cobbles, passing through the sixteenth-century gateway into the Old Town, or Dalt Vila, and circled ever higher through the tiers of buildings to the cathedral. There's been a place of worship here for over two thousand years, since the Phoenicians first built a temple at the highest point. The clubs have been in town fifty years. We made a pact to come back in 4,000 AD and see whether praying or partying had prevailed.

Down at the harbour, we sat on benches under ranks of tall palms and watched the Balearic ferries come and go. In the narrow streets of Sa Penya, under the Dalt Vila hill, a few early-opening T-shirt, music and souvenir stores gamely pretended there were customers by putting up entirely redundant signs saying "No photographs". There were no takers for the bangles, beads and wristbands, and most of the boutiques, bars and restaurants were still closed. Cocktails, Asian fusion, sushi, tacos, gourmet burgers – we'd have to wait another couple of months to dine out on those.

The town market was quiet, and most mornings we were the only people drinking *café con leche* and eating breakfast pastries in the square. It might have been twenty degrees, but the locals were firmly of the opinion that March was far too early to be sitting outdoors. Inside the café, every table was full of people wearing buttoned-up coats, just in case someone opened the door and they got a blast of tepid air.

Spain was trying hard to peep out from under the Ibizan blanket, but it was a struggle. The bars that were open were chilly at night, with not nearly enough customers to generate any heat. Museums and galleries echoed with our solitary footsteps as startled attendants sprang to life at the sound of unexpected guests. It seemed to us that, without the drinkers, the dancers, the clubbers, the beach crowd and the yachties, Ibiza didn't know what to do with itself. And, after a few days, neither did we.

Out of ideas, we stood at a bus-stop one morning and jumped on the next service that came along. It's a small island. You can't go more than thirty kilometres in any direction. It seemed like a risk worth taking.

The bus bumbled through outlying villages, carrying mostly schoolkids and grandmas, and finally stopped at the end of the line, in a small, one-horse town. If it wasn't your turn with the horse, it wasn't obvious what you'd do to pass the time. It was also clear that this was less the cocktail-and-fusion-tapas end of Ibiza and more the furniture-showroom-and-hardware-store side of the island.

We got off the bus and followed a prominent and promising sign that said "Centro". Thirty metres down the town's only street, having run out of shops and buildings, it was clear that we were already very much in the *centro*. Still, there was a church to look at, a brilliant-white-painted one on the top of a small rise at the end of the street. You can always while away time in a Spanish church, lighting the candles, having a kneel on the cushions and counting the gory wounds on the statues.

Naturally, the church was locked. Equally naturally, the return bus wasn't due for three hours.

This might be considered quite annoying. Then again, this was much more like the Spain we were used to. And when you're stuck in middle-of-nowhere Spain in the middle of the day, there's only one thing to do

Lunch.

We walked over to the only restaurant and sat down outside at a plastic table lined with a paper tablecloth. Usually at this point in England we'd be fearing the worst – and expecting a baked potato or toasted sandwich at best – but we were in the Mediterranean and it was lunchtime, and those two things are made for each other.

There followed an entirely jovial but incomprehensible conversation with the waiter, which started with him saying the word "*menú?*"

It's not what you think. If you want the actual, printed menu in a Spanish restaurant, you ask for *la carta*. But at lunchtime you can also choose the *menú del dia*, a bargain, fixed-price, daily deal that offers a limited or no-choice meal designed to keep the workers of Spain fed and happy. They only get four hours off for lunch remember, so they have to fill in the time somehow. In big cities and fashionable places, the deal has been chipped away at over the years. The fixed-price menus are mostly down to two courses and an inclusive glass of wine if you're lucky, but still – for ten or fifteen euros, that's pretty good value.

But down the back alleys of towns and cities, and out in the sticks in Proper Spain, including it seemed, the arse-end of Ibiza, the traditional, full-on, no-holds-barred, *menú del dia* experience still lingers on. The restaurant was full – a novelty on this trip and very reassuring – and no one was bothering the waiter for *la carta*. The diners had come for three courses of whatever was cooking that day and they weren't in any hurry.

Sitting down, we got a cheery welcome – also a novelty on this trip – and then a stream-of-consciousness poetry slam which, from experience, we knew to be the available dishes. These might be written on a blackboard or a bit of paper in some places; here, he was going old-school, off the top of his head. Our limited Spanish was probably no good anyway, the native language of Ibiza being Catalan, which is like Spanish but weirdly different, in the way that you know someone speaking quickly with a strong Geordie accent is still speaking English but not in a manner that you've ever heard before. The waiter's presentation was so fast and furious that it was impossible to tell what was being offered, and the best thing to do in these circumstances is nod randomly whenever there's a pause. It's all food, how bad can it be?

I say that. I suppose it depends on your experience of Spain and Spanish regional food. If you don't speak or understand any Spanish at all, then the rapid-fire *menú del dia* might well lead to you nodding just at the point the waiter has suggested tripe, blood sausage, or bean stew with alarming bits of pig in it. If you hear something that sounds like *fabada* or *cocido*, don't say you haven't been warned. Scoop your spoon around in one of those and it's only a matter of time before you turn up an ear, a snout or worse.

On my first visits to Spain back in the 1980s, as an impecunious backpacker, the *menú del dia* was all part of the learning process. It was uplifting to discover that I could afford to eat well in a restaurant at least once a day. But it was unnerving to find things on my plate that I had never thought of putting in my mouth before. Like blood-red *chorizo* sausage. Or asparagus. Or natural yoghurt for dessert. Who were these people? They'd never be able to get away with serving these outlandish foods in Huddersfield.

Eventually, of course, I came to realise that Spain was right and I was wrong. It turned out that there could be more to lunch than "cheese toastie and salad garnish." I ate and enjoyed squid and suckling pig, chickpeas and spinach, hard sheep's cheese and unctuous ribbons of cured ham, without ever having to do much more than nod or point – safe in the knowledge that whatever turned up was (mostly) as authentic as it got. And if I made the wrong choice or didn't really like the dish, there was always tomorrow's *menú*.

Our Ibizan lunch was a classic of its kind. First up was a tuna salad, big enough on its own as a full meal and served with chunks of chewy fresh bread and a small dish of home-brined olives. This was followed by a butterflied, grilled fish – unidentified, probably seabass – and fried potatoes and more salad, the Spanish view of vegetables other than potato with your main course being that they are only required if you have a doctor's note. The meal finished with a wobbly egg custard sitting in a puddle of caramel sauce.

All in all, nothing too fancy, but all fresh from the market, entirely homemade and delivered to the table on the unspoken understanding that you're going to want three massive courses of food at lunchtime. Which, luckily, we did.

There had been no mention of the price at any point, but that was hardly unusual. It was an all-in budget lunch; no one asks about the price.

There wasn't a question asked about wine either. A bottle simply appeared on everyone's table, because God knows how the rest of the clientele – the builders, the truckers, the office workers – were expected to operate complicated machinery, drive articulated rigs and oversee people's finances and medical procedures without the benefit of a gutsy *vino* at lunchtime.

If you're worried about the cost of the wine, don't be. It wasn't a sneaky upselling ploy to amplify the bill. If a bottle arrives on the table it's included in the price, which took the young travel-writer-me a while to get my head around when I first encountered the practice. Even as a single diner, a bottle of throaty red would appear with the bread at the start of the meal. Well hello Tempranillo. All I would say to my twenty-something self now is that *you don't have to drink it all*. Obviously, you can, and I often did, which is why certain post-lunch-research sections of the *Rough Guide to Spain* are a little hazy on detail. But if they are sticking it on the table for free, it means it's cheap and local, maybe even a top-up from a barrel or wine-box out back, and you don't have to drink it all.

Obviously, we drank it all and then some, because there were two of us and because we still had an hour or so to kill before the bus. There were also two tiny espressos and one giant brandy, or possibly the other way around – and then the bill arrived, almost as an apologetic afterthought.

This isn't one of those travel stories where it turns out that – like rubes in Venice in St Mark's Square – we've misunderstood what's been going on and the bill is actually a thousand euros. I do have stories like that, including a traumatic episode in Hong Kong at a restaurant where I was encouraged to pick a fish from a tank so it could be cooked for me. It was chased around with a little net, scooped up, bashed on the head, steamed to perfection and served on a garnished platter, and tasted absolutely delicious. When the bill came that day, the rice cost a pound, the beer cost a pound and the fish cost sixty pounds, and I actually cried. In public in a restaurant.

Our *menú del día* bill was a ridiculously reasonable thirty-six euros, given that two people were now both stuffed full and drunk. No problem there at all, thirty-six euros very well spent.

The best bit though was the bill itself, because it bore no relation to anything that had been delivered to the table. The torn-off scrap of paper just said "Bar" nine times, and featured completely random amounts, so I kept it as evidence should I ever need to write about how brilliant Ibiza is. If only I could remember what the restaurant was called. Or where the village was. Or indeed how we got back to town. Details, details.

My best guess later was that the *menú* was thirteen or fourteen euros each and the rest was for the extra glass of wine, the coffees and the brandy. And if that seems improbably cheap, you haven't been to back-of-beyond Spain, where an espresso costs a euro and a measure of off-the-shelf Spanish brandy not a whole lot more. That word "measure" does a lot of heavy lifting in Spain, by the way. If the waiter brings the *coñac* bottle to the table to pour, he's waiting for you to say "stop" and you'll blink before a Spanish waiter does. Full-to-the-brim is an entirely acceptable shot of brandy.

So, in the end, we discovered Spain hiding in an out-of-sorts Ibiza, which was just waking up for the summer, rinsing the sleep out of its eyes and getting ready for a long night on the dance floor. By the time everyone else arrived for the season, we'd be long gone – not really our kind of place – but very much looking forward to lunch in whichever corner of Spain we next found ourselves.

A fight over pizza in Italy

WHO COOKS THE best dough, tomatoes and cheese – that's the only question you need to ask to start a proper argument in Naples.

I dare say other subjects would do. Was Maradona the best footballer that ever lived? (The locally correct answer is "yes"). Is it nicer in Rome? (That would be a "no"). But if you're looking for an operatic shouting match bordering on a brawl, then really you just need to stop a group of locals and ask them which is the best pizzeria in town.

I came to Naples looking for an answer to that very question and, if you keep reading, it will all be worth it. I'm not going to sit on the fence. You'll end up with the name and address of the best pizzeria in Naples, which is no mean thing to have. But oh boy, the drama of it; the song and dance; the rigmarole involved in finding out. I don't see why I should give up the information just like that. So buckle up, and let's begin at the beginning.

For a start, you might be thinking, why Naples? But that's because you're not Neapolitan. If you are, the question would not compute. Even if you're just generally Italian or of Italian descent, you're going – albeit grudgingly – to give this one to the *napoletani*.

It's this. Pizza is best in Naples, Italy. It just is.

I know, you've had brilliant ones in New York City, London or Melbourne, perhaps even Naples, Florida, and maybe you hold your local pizza joint in extremely high regard. But modern pizza was born in Naples, which – by definition – makes the mystical quest for the city's best pizza also a search for the best pizza in the world. That's why I was in Naples, looking for the planet's finest tomato- and cheese-topped dough and, as with all the best quests, there were challenges aplenty ahead.

By the way, I'm skating over the tendentious history here, because we don't have all day. The ancient Egyptians and Greeks made flatbreads, long before anyone else got in on the act. Babylonians, Persians, Etruscans, Romans – they all added stuff to the top of baked dough. The Turks still do and call it *pide*; even the French claim a version called *pissaladière*. You could make a case for any or all of these being the precursor to the pizza, but none of it matters because the thing we recognise unequivocally today as a pizza emerged in Naples, probably around three hundred years ago.

Not even in Italy, note, because Italy has only really been a single, unified country since 1861. Nope, this is Naples' gig and it's best just to get on board with that now, because it saves a lot of arguments later on.

So if you're looking for the best pizza in the world, you have to go to Naples. Like you'd hit up France for the champagne.

Or Spain for the *jamón ibérico*. Or England for … well there must be something, but you get the idea. Which leads to the first challenge, which is that Naples has a certain image problem that often puts people off visiting.

It's not immediately attractive, like Rome or the Tuscan towns. It doesn't, on first viewing, even seem particularly Italian in the hackneyed, stereotypical way you might expect Italian cities to be. It's a bit gruff, unkempt and abrupt, a sort of sweary tramp to Rome's cool hipster. If you've never been, Googling for information doesn't help – suggested questions and answers under "Naples" include "Why is it so dirty?", "Is it dangerous?" and "Is it safe to walk around?" When Bill Bryson came, he was appalled by the din and the filth and didn't even stay the night. It's also no help that the most famous quotation attached to the city – "See Naples and die" – sounds like a threat, rather than the eighteenth-century hymn to the city's erstwhile grandeur that it started out as.

You really don't need to worry. It does take a bit of getting used to, but Naples unfolds its own charms over time.

As I thundered into the historic centre in a taxi, initial impressions were of narrow, canyon-like streets of towering buildings. Fleeting initial impressions, I should say. The driver threw the car around in the manner of Harrison Ford piloting the *Millennium Falcon* on the Kessel Run. Twelve parsecs from train station to hotel was no problem for this guy. We scattered pedestrians who had the temerity to be walking on the pavements and squeezed through the skinniest of alleys at high speed, metalwork just centimetres from walls and bollards. He screeched to a halt in a tiny square, looked round as if to say "Ta-da!" and extracted from his dazed passenger a probably highly inflated amount in euros before roaring away again.

I spent the next couple of days getting my bearings. Naples has some literal high points, where you can get a view of the city, the bay and Vesuvius beyond, and also a seafront promenade of sorts. There's a castle or three and an old royal palace. The archaeological museum is fabulous. You could certainly sightsee, if that's what you were here for.

But the centre itself is a connected series of crowded, historic neighbourhoods that never really feels like it opens up and breathes. Those canyon-like streets are repeated in confusing patterns, and charming, fountain-centred piazzas in the Audrey Hepburn-*Roman Holiday* vein are thin on the ground. Towering, barrel-arched gateways lead into neighbourhoods of high tenements, with washing strung across balconies and ball games in the street. Street art and graffiti cover every wall and shuttered shop-front. Literally every wall. It's close, confined and hemmed-in; you'll round a corner and there's the elaborately carved doorway to an otherwise unannounced church, its spire or bell-tower impossible to see from the narrow street, however much you crane your neck. The pock-marked buildings are grey-black with age and traffic pollution; the markets might have been worm-holed in from the Middle Ages with their chicken-feet sellers, blanket vendors and one-legged beggars.

You can see why people think it's unsafe, but in truth Naples is just fine. I mean, obviously don't stand in the street waving cash, or ask an urchin to take a photo of you with your iPhone. My hotel did go to great pains to make sure I knew to keep my bag zipped and in view at all times, but it's not like they sent me out under armed guard or anything. All this is to say that if you are on the hunt for great pizza – the greatest of pizza – you will have to be prepared to walk down streets that look a bit sketchy at times. But that's just Naples; the whole place looks a bit sketchy.

The people are hilarious, in the best possible way. The taxi driver was not a unique specimen of his trade – crossing a road at an official pedestrian crossing, with the green man and beeping signal, simply brings down the full, indignant wrath of every imprecation-yelling taxi driver within horn-tooting distance. I watched one driver reverse at speed from a side road into oncoming traffic on a busy highway. As cars, trucks and buses careered around him – blazing horns, shaking fists and questioning his parentage – he was not in the slightest abashed, suggesting instead through his open window, with clear hand gestures, that he saw his careful and considered driving as very much everyone else's problem.

It's not just the drivers either. My first *al fresco* lunch – at a busy road intersection, with cars brushing the tablecloth – featured a stand-up row with the waiter who had clearly forgotten my order. When queried, after about forty-five minutes, he simultaneously denied he'd ever seen me before and then said the thing I had apparently not ordered was *finito*, before flouncing back into the restaurant muttering the word *inglese* (English) a lot, together with many more words that I didn't know. In case of doubt, it's best to work on the assumption that in Naples the customer is never right.

Somewhere though – in those, dark, tight, cramped streets – comically furious Neapolitans were cooking the finest circular, oven-baked dishes known to humanity. I went to work.

At some time in the eighteenth century, it's thought, what you might recognise as a modern pizza first made its appearance in Naples. They were probably sold from stalls, deep in these self-same streets, and there's even a candidate for the very first, the Antica Pizzeria Port'Alba, founded by street-sellers in 1738 and a bricks-and-mortar restaurant since 1830. That makes it the oldest pizzeria in Naples (and thus Italy, and the world, etc), and I sat outside one night at a pavement table in a slightly quieter and less frenetic part of the old town. The waiter said there was no carafe of house wine available, even though the next table had just that, brought me a pricier bottle and then eventually delivered the pizza once he'd finished talking to his girlfriend on the phone. Despite all that, I'm duty bound to report that the Antica Pizzeria is pretty good and worth a visit – but it's not the best pizza in the city.

Come the nineteenth century, pizza makers were establishing themselves as chefs and acquiring reputations. Although it had probably been around as a combination for decades already, the tomato, mozzarella and basil topping was made famous in 1889 by the great Naples pizza chef, or *pizzaiolo*, Raffaele Esposito. He named this most basic of pizzas the *margherita*, in honour of the Queen of Italy, Margherita of

Savoy – the ingredients being red, white and green, the colours of the national flag.

Basic but beloved – it's the *margherita* and its cheese-less cousin, the *marinara* (tomatoes, garlic, oil and oregano), that are the staples in Naples. (I've been waiting to use that.) Once I'd got to grips with the local preferences, there was only one place to go. Founded in 1870, the back-street Pizzeria da Michele serves these two pizzas and nothing else. Literally the only choice is whether or not you want the *margherita* to come with double mozzarella. (I think you do.) Drinks? Beer, water or Coke. That's it.

Fortunately for them, if not for the rest of us, the place featured in Elizabeth Gilbert's *Eat Pray Love*, where she has a *When Harry Met Sally*, "I'll have what she's having," moment with her pizza; Julia Roberts recreated the scene here on location in the film version. Consequently, getting a table involves acquiring a numbered ticket from the desk, standing outside in a frenzied crowd, recognising the Italian number when it's shouted, and fighting through said crowd before someone else nabs your table. Once inside, it's not exactly romantic-dinner-for-two territory either; it's simple, loud and brusque and you'll be in and out quicker than you can say Eat Pay Shove. I persevered – you may not, no judgement – and the verdict is that the pizza here was fabulous and ridiculously cheap. But it's still not the best pizza in the city.

If only there was an organisation devoted to codifying the rules for preparing authentic Neapolitan pizza and bestowing a charter-mark upon selected restaurants; that would surely help

170

in the quest for the best pizza in the world, said literally no one ever, especially in Italy where rules and regulations are more on the advisory side and not things to live your life by.

But so seriously are pizzas taken in Naples that there is such an organisation – the *Associazione Verace Pizza Napoletana* (AVPN), which judges what is and what isn't a true, original, *pizza napoletana*. Founded in 1984, the AVPN has over eight hundred accredited members worldwide, scores and scores of them in Naples alone, all adjudged to serve an authentic pizza that meets their strict criteria.

If I thought this would help, I was wrong.

The rules alone run to fourteen pages of closely typewritten text. They are extraordinarily specific and exacting, ranging from the weight of the dough balls used (between two hundred and two hundred and eighty grammes) to the height of the raised edge of the cooked pizza (no more than one to two centimetres). The raised border even has an official name, the *cornicione*. The dough has to be fashioned by hand and the ingredients have to come from the local Campania region – hand-crushed San Marzano tomatoes, the cheese either *mozzarella di bufala campana* or *fior di latte*, cold-pressed extra virgin olive oil, and fresh basil leaves. Hundreds of words are devoted to the fermentation process of the dough. There are step-by-step instructions for the exact amount of salt required, or the spiralling method used for applying sauce and oil. And all this is before you even get to the art of slipping the pizza into a traditional, domed, wood-fired oven (burning only oak, ash, beech or maple) at a temperature of four hundred and eighty-five degrees Celsius for a maximum of ninety seconds.

Do all this properly and your restaurant too can display the "Vera Pizza Napoletana" sticker, which you'd think would narrow things down. But it doesn't, because every fecker in town has the sticker. It's a bold pizza restaurant in Naples that doesn't apply for AVPN accreditation, though I suppose there are gangs of ironic young hipsters who meet up at the sticker-free establishments with badly cooked pizza because everywhere else is just so mainstream, man.

It's really simple, I whined to my hotel, I only want to know which is the best pizzeria, serving the best pizza. I'd tried the Port'Alba and Da Michele, and a handful of others, each of them wonderful in its way. Like Di Matteo, another old-school establishment where they take a *calzone* and they fry it – yes they do, they fold and fry a pizza, just because. It's magnificent, and the oil and juices stain your hands and drip down your clothes, but it's still not the best pizza in the city.

Have you tried Pizzeria Sorbillo, they said, or rather whispered, because stating out loud that they thought it was the best could only lead to an argument, and they were in the hospitality rather than the street-shouting business.

I wandered down to Via dei Tribunali to check it out and, like most of the other good places in Naples, it was nothing much to look at, inside or out. It's been there since 1935, with the Sorbillo family still in charge, but the décor budget has remained largely untroubled during that time. The pizza appeared astonishingly quickly – I'd say it spent closer to sixty than ninety seconds in the oven, which was in full view of the diners, but I'm assuming that was allowed in the regs. Everything else was as per the rules – tomatoes, cheese, the *cornicione*, bubbled and slightly blackened, a slick of good oil, an arrangement of freshly torn basil leaves.

Now that was excellent. Clouds-open, shaft-of-light, celestial-harmonics excellent. This, surely, was it?

I came back one more time for verification purposes and I'm prepared to call it for Sorbillo. Both *margherita* and *marinara* are stonkingly good. They use the same ingredients as everyone else, but they squeeze just a morsel more taste and pizzaz from them, which seems like a suitable word to use for a pizza. They must have their methods, a special way of manipulating the dough perhaps, but their website is no help – "The secret of the pizza is a secret," it says.

Unlike the hairshirt hardliners at Da Michele, there are a few other things that Sorbillo allow on a pizza – salami and onions, for example, or ricotta and zucchini – but if you're looking for sweetcorn, pineapple or barbecued chicken, you are *so* going to be in the wrong place. I'm not sure there is actually anything else on the menu – no appetisers, no salads, no mains, no fries. For drinks, you can either have a beer or you can have a tiny aircraft-style bottle of wine for one. You can have a really tiny espresso coffee at the end. The whole experience won't take long. You'll be in and out in under an hour.

By now, this shouldn't sound disappointing. These limitations are strengths. Less is more. All that. Eating at Sorbillo is one of the planet's most extraordinary restaurant experiences. It is very reasonably priced. You don't need to book weeks or months in advance. You don't even need to speak Italian.

So there, eventually, it is.

Pizzeria Sorbillo on Via dei Tribunali. The best pizza in Naples, Italy, the World, the Universe, and, heck why not, the whole darn Multiverse. You're welcome.

A view to die for in Montenegro

LET'S SAY YOU'RE looking for a place to put down roots and call home. How about this strategically sited hillside overlooking the southern Adriatic, handy for sea access and trade?

It's protected by the mountains behind and has an early-warning view down across the plain to the ocean. Great location, looks nice and safe, and can be easily defended – all you need to do is just build some walls and towers between the forbidding crags. Climate's not half bad either. There's fresh spring water, while olives, figs, vines, pomegranates and peaches grow in abundance. Why wouldn't you want to live here?

Unfortunately for the original inhabitants of Bar – who settled the place in 800 BC, maybe even earlier – pretty much everyone thought the same thing.

Illyrians, Greeks and Celts all passed through on trading expeditions, while pirates often attempted to take it but failed. The Romans definitely took a liking to it, as the name attests. Whatever its earliest inhabitants called the town is not recorded. Instead, it's known as Bar, a shortened form of the Latin

Antibarium, named as such because it sat across the Adriatic from the old Roman town of *Barium* (now Bari in Italy).

Once the Empire fell, Bar's favoured trade routes were up for grabs by a motley selection of tribes and kingdoms. The town sat for a while under Byzantine rule, before being knocked around for several more centuries by assorted Slavs, Venetians and Ottomans. It did eventually become part of Montenegro in 1878, though unfortunately only by being liberated – oh, all right then, blown up – by heavy artillery. It was bombed again in both world wars and, to cap it all, anything that was left standing was then given another good going over by a devastating earthquake in 1979.

That would explain the ruins on the hillside then. And why there's a modern city of Bar, down on the coast, where everyone now lives. It's an hour from the capital, Podgorica, on the train – pleasant enough but hardly an essential visit. But the shattered old town – up in the hills, in the place now known as Stari Bar, or "Old Bar" – well that's a different matter, still with a tale to tell.

Home sweet home? Hardly. Ghost town, archaeological site, tourist attraction? It's all three and something more besides – a monument to the lengths people will go to grab something that isn't theirs, and a reminder of the ultimate power of nature that cares not a jot about any of that.

Within the encircling walls and battlements of the old town, visitors now pay a couple of euros to wander the tree-shaded cobbled alleys and streets, peering into collapsed buildings and clambering across piles of rubble that were once houses, shops, squares and thoroughfares. Over many centuries, several thousand people called Stari Bar home – when it was just Bar, when there was nothing 'old' about it. And as people do, they lived their lives and adapted to new rules and ways with every changed circumstance, seeing fortress walls raised and churches converted to mosques.

In part, it's a melancholic experience. That it should come to this, for proud Bar – to be yoked to the tourist dollar and packaged as a tumbledown historic sight. There are worse fates though – just ask the current inhabitants of living, breathing Kotor and Dubrovnik, who continue about their daily lives as best they can amid the swarming crowds vomited from towering cruise ships.

At least here in derelict Bar there are no locals to get in the way of and annoy, no life to interrupt. You have the space to use your imagination, as you scramble across the ruined thresholds of houses where families once lived and children played. If there are ghosts here, they seem content to be disturbed by the occasional visitor that strays up the side alleys and investigates the mounds of fallen masonry.

The Montenegrin Pompeii, some call it, and there's certainly a superficial resemblance. Crumbling houses facing streets that go nowhere; foundations and floor plans that refuse to give up their mystery; wildflowers spreading through heaped stones; empty windows framing isolated walls and distant views. Candles outside a restored church flicker in the gentle hillside breeze, and red-faced visitors sit under the shade of ancient trees that have been allowed to spread and grow in the shattered spaces.

Unlike Pompeii, however, there's no sense that life just stopped moments ago. No embalmed lovers entwined; no ancient, graffitied shop counters; no surviving mosaics, frescoes or sculpted adornments. Bar was hit by a cataclysmic event, it's true, but not one that buried a town but rather comprehensively flattened it.

Under Ottoman control, Bar held out during a siege by Montenegrin forces in 1877, suffering artillery bombardment for week after week. Eventually, the Montenegrins tired of trying to persuade Bar that its future lay with them and they blew the town's aqueduct sky high, cutting off the water supply. The town surrendered in January 1878 but never fully revived its fortunes, stumbling on for another century until the 1979 earthquake finished it off for good.

Consequently, it's hard to make sense of the vine-clad ruins and broken buildings, though some have been reconstructed and others have simple explanations attached. Paths and signs point you round the site – past a bathhouse, clocktower, chapels, wells, arches and aqueduct – while climbing to the fortress walls gives you grandstand views down to the modern city of Bar and the sparkling sea beyond.

This is where you understand, perhaps for the first time, why so many armies marched up the hill and down again. To own this place, this site, this dramatic location, must have been a powerful lure from the first day it was settled. It would confer status, it would guarantee prosperity, and it would secure a future for your people.

Aside from a small museum and a restored building or two, there's no development inside the walls, though outside is a different matter. The steep street up from the taxi stand and bus stop is lined with souvenir stands, cafés and restaurants. Modern Bar – way below – is creeping back up, as the descendants of those who abandoned the old town in the first place realise that there are pickings to be had from the increasing number of tourists. It's still on a fairly manageable scale, and largely good humoured, though again – ask Kotor or Dubrovnik – it's surely only a matter of time before garden bars sprout within the walls and enterprising entrepreneurs turn battered buildings into boutique B&Bs.

For now, though, despite the continual daily influx of visitors through the grand fortified gate, it's still possible to escape the crowds. Move away from the pinch points, explore beyond the main streets, peer into roofless rooms and clamber into hidden chambers – it's here that you can really lose yourself among the whispers and memories of the lost city.

Meanwhile, in Kaldrma, a simple restaurant on the steep main street, visitors sit on a pretty vine-covered terrace and eat traditional dishes such as baked garlic aubergine, roast lamb, and stuffed vine leaves. The slow-food approach extends itself to the service, but after a long lunch here and a saunter through the ruins of Stari Bar you begin to realise that time is measured differently in a place of such antiquity.

If you needed any more evidence of this, it comes with the short taxi ride from the old town back to Bar station by way of Mirovica. Set in a ring of white stones is a spreading olive tree of gargantuan proportions, said to be over two thousand five hundred years old. While you don't have to buy the bold claim – "the world's oldest olive tree" – the symbolism is irresistible. Where better to call home than a place where olive saplings take root, on a sunny Adriatic hillside with unparalleled views down to the ocean? This will do, this is where we'll live, and our town will last as long as the olive trees grow.

A quest for a perfect pint in Ireland

THE FIRST PERSON who ever poured me a Guinness was dressed in a nurse's uniform, while I lay largely undressed and prone in bed one night.

Hang on, let me have another go. My mother might read this.

The first person who ever poured me a Guinness was a nurse. It used to be the case that hospital patients in England were offered a glass of Guinness on evening rounds because, as the advertising made clear, it was good for you. Full of antioxidants apparently, plus the alcohol of course, which they seemingly weren't too bothered about, because they even gave it to pregnant women. I got a glass and I'd only had my wisdom teeth out. Half a pint for that, a pint for a broken leg, and so on up to a skin-full depending on your affliction – I think that was the policy, though I was a bit sketchy on the details having had a general anaesthetic and all four impacted wisdom teeth removed with pliers by a large man kneeling on my chest. When my friends came to visit after the operation, they walked right past my bed because the only person they could see was –

in their words – "That fright in the corner with the face like an over-inflated chipmunk."

It was another ten years before I had my first proper Guinness, not through a straw in hospital but in a glass in Dublin. I'd drunk plenty of pints that passed as Guinness by then, mostly in England but also in places like Barcelona and Hong Kong, but as any Irish person will tell you – and you'll regret getting them started – they were not proper pints. And to be fair, as the Guinness in Hong Kong, for example, had been downed in an Australian bar accompanied by a band of Filipino musicians playing English trad jazz by way of New Orleans, I could see their point. By the way, don't even mention to an Irish person that you had a Guinness in an "Irish Pub" in Malaga or Malibu; there'll only be a narrowing of the eyes and a sorry shake of the head.

The beer doesn't travel well, that's what I'm told, like Guinness is an elderly aunt in a headscarf shivering in the deck-side breeze, rather than a velvet punch in a glass that can cure any ailment known to the NHS. No, it's a thin and sour affair, the Guinness in England, not to be trusted. Plus, apparently, we pour it in the wrong manner and serve it at the wrong temperature in the wrong glasses. And we're English, don't forget that. Stiff upper lip, no soul, none of the exuberant generosity that marks out and compliments a person as *flaithulach* ("flahooluck"). Too busy with the imperialism and the colonising to appreciate properly a rare drop of the black stuff, a drink that the great Irish writer and humourist Flann O'Brien called "The Workman's Friend." A dark stout, a porter, a beer, when it comes to solving your problems said O'Brien, "A pint of plain is your only man." What could the English know of all this?

"There you go anyway," said the Irish barman in Scruffy Murphy's, "that'll be six pounds thirty."

I bought the *terroir* argument, why not? Like French claret or New Zealand Pinot Noir, I was prepared to believe that Guinness tasted better in Ireland because of the peculiar alchemy of water, weather and ingredients. They've been making it since 1759; they probably know what they're doing. As for the rest, we'd see, but the Guinness was calling me to Dublin.

If the Irish are very firm on the subject of where you shouldn't drink Guinness – basically, England – then Dubliners are equally adamant about where you shouldn't drink it – basically, Temple Bar. It's a place, not a pub, the party zone by the south side of the River Liffey, where tourists roam in search of the real Ireland, pursuing the mythical *craic* down a few unkempt streets and back alleys. Not "the crack" by the way. Dubliners laugh uproariously if you tell them you went out on the crack in Temple Bar. We foreigners have the concept entirely wrong. *Craic* is a dynamic life force, the word a multi-layered appreciation of fun, gossip, sociability, camaraderie and good conversation – not specifically attached to binge-drinking Guinness, as every foreigner thinks it is, but then not excluding it either, if that will lead to fun, gossip, sociability, camaraderie and good conversation.

"That was great *craic* last night," Irish people might reasonably say, about an evening spent entirely around the kitchen table drinking hot chocolate together and going to bed at ten o'clock. Equally, "Ah jaysus, the *craic*" could apply to a night spent strapped to a lamp post in a mankini.

Anyway, no Dubliner would go out on the crack in Temple Bar, but as they don't tell you that at the entry ports, I wasted my first ever true Irish Guinness experience in a pub filled to bursting with English stag and hen parties. I was seduced by the green panelling, the faux-vintage lettering, the harps, shamrocks and fiddle music – all the Oirish paddywhackery, in fact, that marks out a bar in Dublin as not a proper pub. How toasty was the barley and creamy the head of that first pint? What depth the flavour, how smooth the linger? Difficult to say, with Dutch backpackers, American students and lairy young women in uniform (not, I suspect, real nurses) barging shoulders, spilling drinks and bellowing out approximate renditions of "The Irish Rover" in the wrong key.

Not to worry, there were lots more pubs in Dublin and, by definition, being in Dublin, all of them served better Guinness than at home. Really, the quest was for a better pub and not a better pint.

I asked around, and then over the next few days, and subsequently the next few visits, I started to walk, which is never a bad idea in Dublin. The handsome Georgian terraces and squares are famous, and the grey river cutting through the middle is a useful aide when it comes to finding your way around. You switch from the Ramblas-like O'Connell Street to warren-like back alleys in a matter of minutes and are never far from an elegant façade or a cheeky statue. I like a city where there's a monument to two un-named women doing their shopping ("The hags with the bags," if you're asking for directions) *and* to Phil Lynott, yer man with the bass and big hair from Thin Lizzie.

There's also a statue of James Joyce, of course ("The prat with the hat" – the Irish are no respecter of status), whose work hangs heavy over Dublin. Let's face it, the story told in *Ulysses* is essentially of one big walk around the city that takes place on the sixteenth of June, 1904; "Bloomsday", as it's known, is celebrated each year with tours, events and visits to every place namechecked in the novel. Start with Joyce then, you'd think, if it's Dublin pubs you're after, which means starting with Davy Byrne's, the bar where the novel's protagonist, Leopold Bloom, goes for lunch on his one-day odyssey around the city.

It looks the part, you have to give it that, with its gleaming Art Deco interior – and it is just around the corner from Big Phil Lynott, so you've done a bit of sightseeing already and earned a pint. However, the problem with Davy Byrne's is that Joyce didn't know what he was talking about regarding the Guinness. Good on the old modernist literature and writing Ireland's greatest masterpiece, can't fault him there; a bit suspect on drinks and drinking. Joyce doesn't have Leopold Bloom come in Davy Byrne's for a pint of plain. Instead, he has him order a glass of burgundy and a Gorgonzola cheese sandwich, which they still serve up today if you insist. Let's not forget that Joyce was in charge here, doing the writing. He could have made it a Guinness, that's all I'm saying, it would have made more sense.

And another thing. When he wrote about Guinness at all, Joyce called it "the frothy freshener," which suggests, at least to me, that he'd never had a pint of it in his life. I can think of many words you'd use to describe Guinness before reaching for "frothy" – creamy, velvety, buttery, silky, smooth, soothing, lush. Froth is a wispy, insubstantial foam. Guinness, body and head combined, is more in the way of a dense, ambrosial cream that, in other circumstances, you might slap on a cake or use to fill cavity walls. It fills, it satisfies, and rather than freshening, four or five pints of it is just as likely to put you in the sort of coma that requires defibrillator paddles to get you started again.

Let's be fair to Davy Byrne's though, they do a decent pint of Guinness and, what's more, you can have it old-school, served with half a dozen oysters and some Guinness-infused soda bread. That's better than a bag of crisps any day. But the pub was busy with tourists ordering red wine and cheese sandwiches, and didn't have the atmosphere I was looking for. I wasn't ready to call off the search just yet.

What follows could be described as a pub crawl of what I eventually determined were central Dublin's finest pubs, but fair warning – you wouldn't do them in this order, and if you drank a pint in each one you'd be pretty ill the next day. While I'm breaking the fourth wall here, I might as well be upfront about it. I've been to Dublin many times since I first had a duff pint in Temple Bar. I've done the legwork so you don't have to, but

I've also constructed a story about it, so I've chosen pubs that fit the narrative. As long as we're all cool with that, here we go.

The first proper Guinness I had in a real Dublin pub was in the Palace Bar, a Victorian delight of mahogany and mirrors that can be rammed to the rafters at four in the afternoon just as easily as ten at night.

Here I learned two more essential truths about Guinness. The first is that, unlike England, it's really the only beer in town, by which I mean you can go into any pub in Ireland and say, "I'll have a pint" and they'll automatically fetch you a Guinness. They won't look askance and ask whether you mean lager or bitter, artisan IPA or fizzy keg, because why would they? They have your only man, a pint of plain, right here, in abundance.

The second is that you need to allow time, because it turns out that every Irish barman complaining about the crap Guinness served abroad is absolutely correct. From first pour to pint in hand could be anything up to ten minutes, and I'm not kidding. It's not a drink to order if you've a raging thirst. They pour it into a glass up to about halfway, then go away and deal with some more customers while the creamy goodness settles; then they come back and pour a bit more in, and then go away again, sometimes on holiday or at least on a short city break, before coming back for the final time, pulling up a chair, finishing *Ulysses* and lazily topping off your thick, luscious pint with a palette knife. Clever bar staff in busy pubs have a line of half-filled Guinness glasses on the go at any one time, so that new punters only have to wait until their next birthday for a pint.

The Palace is little more than a corridor-length bar punctuated by carved wooden screens, with a lip of wood down the other side of the room where you can rest your drink. It's beautiful, in that High Victorian, dimly lit way of vintage city pubs, but it's shoulder-to-shoulder at times. I pushed my way through with my hard-won pint and saw what everybody had meant when they said, "Make sure you see the back bar, it's grand." This is the place to savour a drop of Guinness on a first or fiftieth visit, on wooden chairs at battered tables, under a vaulted, stained-glass skylight, surrounded by portraits of Dublin's literati from bygone days.

That's one pint down.

A friend put me on to Grogan's – full of shabby dodgers, he said, and writers and artists, and people pretending to be writers and artists. And for Chrissake, don't look too longingly at any of the art on the walls, he added, they might try and sell it to you. But have a cheese toastie, they're great. And the Guinness is top drawer. This brief summary turned out to be right on all counts, so good call. It's another of those old literary hangouts – this was Flann O'Brien's favourite and, as we know, he's to be more trusted on the matter than Joyce, so good man yourself O'Brien.

Two.

Next up is the Stag's Head, which is a grand place for a few scoops, featuring yet another glorious Victorian interior of burnished and carved wood, polished marble and gleaming mirrors. The granite pillars at the entrance make it look like a bank and the stained glass inside is worthy of a cathedral, but it's extraordinarily cosy – never has a "snug" bar been more aptly named. It's suspiciously close to Temple Bar and there is live music, but the Stag's ring of authenticity keeps you and your Guinness safe from the flailing arms of lashed-up lads from Liverpool.

Best of all though is its proximity to the letterbox-red Dame Tavern, right opposite. If you can't get in one, you can try the other. Or both. Or stand on the pavements between the two with hundreds of other people, drinking perfect Guinness. I loved the Dame from the off, with its promise of "Guinness. Horses. Music. Craic." Who could resist? (There are no actual horses you understand. It's horse-racing on the TV. Just so you're not disappointed.) It's also probably the darkest pub in the world, so don't put your Guinness down, you'll never find it again.

That's four pints by now. How's it going? I think we need food. Luckily, it's not far to O'Neill's, which is the one with the clock over the entrance, just across from the Molly Malone statue, so it's easy to find. Yes, "The tart with the cart;" I told you, Dubliners are not subtle when it comes to nicknaming landmarks. There's also "The floozie in the jacuzzi" – a reclining female figure in a pond – and "The pole in the hole," which is about the least offensive of the names given to the soaring metal spire on O'Connell Street.

Anyway, find Molly Malone – "The dish with the fish," they can keep this up all day – and you'll find O'Neill's. It's a genuine hotchpotch of rooms in a three-hundred-year-old building, all on different levels, so the best advice is to rope yourself together if you've had a few. Finding a space in here is like negotiating the cramped quarters of an eighteenth-century frigate while it pitches and rolls in a Force Eight off the Cape. Let's leave the Guinness out of it, because it's good, of course it is, it's in Dublin. We're here for the food, which is served in the sort of portions that a pressganged sailor might appreciate, and once we've got that down we'll be grand for the final flourish.

Five pints, is it?

We'll make it half a dozen – nice round number – in the one true pub, the one pub to rule them all, The Long Hall. Here, in one of the oldest bars in the city, I first found Guinness Ground Zero and have never yet discovered a better pint in a better Dublin pub.

It has an unparalleled Victorian boozer's interior – when stained glass, chandeliers, mirrors and mahogany panelling were deemed just the right kind of décor for the working man to be surrounded by while enjoying his drink. The Long Hall has been handcrafted, inlaid, gold-leafed, embossed and bevelled to within an inch of its life, while the high stools down the lengthy bar offer a view of pint-pullers extraordinaire, turning out creamy draught after creamy draught. There are tourists and out-of-towners, it's a well-known place. But there's no music, no dancing and no telly, and the person on the next bar stool is as likely to be on their way home from work as on holiday. There is, most definitely, *craic* to be had of the proper and authentic kind.

Number six? Shall we?

Let's allow Joyce to decide, he owes us a pint, and while he's no good on the Guinness, he knows his stuff when it comes to writing last lines. Here he is in *Ulysses*, at the end of a stream of consciousness hundreds of pages long that has just changed the course of literary history.

Will you have that last pint, James, here with us in The Long Hall?

"Yes I said yes I will Yes."

A place to call home on Planet Earth

I WAS BORN, as you know, in Ghana, West Africa, and I grew up in Huddersfield, West Yorkshire. It was Dad's fault, both times, and I was only shy of him being offered a job in the West Indies to have completed the hat-trick.

My father was hugely well-travelled, mostly on account of his job as a technical specialist in overseas education – or "teacher," if you will – which took him to forty-seven different countries during his career. You could say I caught the travel bug from him, though of course it never seemed like that at the time, what with me being a child and then a teenager and him being Dad and therefore very annoying and embarrassing. Until much later in life, the only travelling we did together was on family holidays, where whatever wide-eyed wonderment he derived from adventurously roaming the globe was curtailed by the pressing need to find a restaurant where his ingrate children wouldn't complain about the food.

I'd like to say that I was inspired in my own travels by the memories of father and young son, hand in hand, gazing on a sunset over Lake Como, or eating mussels in a sunny square in

Perpignan, to take two places that I know we went. The stand-out memory, however, is of my sister and I being allowed to push the wine-laden trolley in a Calais hypermarket en route home and crashing it into the back of his ankles. There must be a whole cohort of French fifty-somethings in the Pas de Calais region who can recall where they first learned a new and colourful selection of English words together with the striking phrase, "You pair of bloody clowns." See. Annoying, embarrassing.

Although Dad was away a lot when we were growing up – weeks or even months at a time – the biggest compliment I can pay both my parents is that we never really noticed. Obviously, we were children and we had school, our rabbit, our bikes and the TV. I don't imagine it was quite so plain-sailing for Mum, left at home to look after two pre-teens while Dad frolicked in the Seychelles or Fiji; sorry, I meant showed slides about educational theory to engineering grad students for about an hour a day before sloping off to the beach for a cocktail with a little umbrella in it. But as far as we were concerned, we used to wave him off one day and then look back up from *Here Come the Double Deckers* another and say "Oh, hi Dad."

Despite all the travel, and the forty-seven countries, we weren't army brats or expat kids, forever on the move. After returning from Ghana, with me in tow, Dad first got a job in Birkenhead, near Liverpool, and then in Melbourn, which Mum was doubtless relieved to learn was near Cambridge and not in Australia. (Let's be fair, he'd already come home at least once before and said "Guess where I've got a job, go on, where do you think?", safe in the knowledge that she was never going to get "Africa" on the first guess. Even if he'd given her "G" as a clue – Grantham? Gillingham? – it was going to be a while before she got to Ghana.)

In fact, after I was born, Mum and Dad only lived in three places, in four different houses, all in England, the last of which was Huddersfield, which remained their home together for forty-eight years – Mum still lives there today. He might have been to the far ends of the earth – this is a man who once flew around Mount Everest – but Dad very definitely had a place to call home, and it was a green valley under a hill on the edge of an old textile town in West Yorkshire.

Places I've lived in the same period? Twelve, in five countries and twenty-two different houses. I think it's safe to say that I've never really had a place I call home.

Huddersfield is where I grew up. It's where I lived for the longest uninterrupted time in my life – thirteen years, until I left home for college – but it's not my home. It's not a bad town; there are worse places – Hell, Hull and Halifax, to name three, if you're paying attention. But I didn't choose it, Dad did, along with Mum. I don't come from there, any more than I come from Ghana – not really, not in the sense people mean. I don't stay anywhere long enough. I don't put down roots. I don't really come from anywhere and I'm running out of time to find the kind of home they had. Put it like this. I'm not now going to live in a single place for forty-eight years, not unless that whole body-replacement technology moves on a bit quicker. Or home cryogenics becomes a thing. Elaine can keep me in the freezer, un-thaw me when the climate's gone to pot and Yorkshire warms up a bit.

I thought about this on the way to the hospital, and then again as I stood in the ward, looking out of the window, down on Huddersfield and right the way across town to the stone memorial tower on Castle Hill. It's a famous local landmark, built in 1899 to honour Queen Victoria, who I'm sure was touched. It's the thought that counts. You see the tower on any drive into Huddersfield. Mum and Dad must have noticed Castle Hill the day they first arrived, and then they bought a house under its skirts and lived there together for forty-eight years.

From his bed, Dad couldn't see the tower, but he had other things on his mind anyway.

"That bloke over there" – he pointed across the ward – "isn't ill. He's swinging the lead."

First, shush, everyone can hear you. And second, what on earth are you on about, Father? The bloke in question was hooked up to at least two drips and was flat on his back, immobile. He was the colour of a wet bank holiday Monday on the Yorkshire coast and looked about as cheery.

"He had a visitor and I heard him say that he was just pretending. He said there was nothing wrong with him, but he wasn't going to tell the nurses because it was free board and lodging."

Right. Well, unlikely, but I suppose you never know.

Then there was a new tack.

"I went out last night, did I tell you?"

195

I looked at Dad.

"How do you mean?"

"It was a concert. At the theatre in town. The doctors took me. Took all of us, you know, an outing. I got dressed and we went to the concert and then I got back here some time in the night."

"You went out? Last night?"

"To a concert, yes, I just said."

This seemed even less likely, but again, who knows? I'd only just arrived; I wasn't yet up to speed with his medical care and the hospital outings policy. I tried to pin him down on some details, but by then we had moved on to other subjects – my work, the hospital food, when he thought he might be able to go home. Home, in the valley, under the hill, just there, out the window, close enough to touch.

I found out later it was the morphine talking.

I mean, it could have just been Dad being Dad. Both things he had said sounded unlikely, but they were fundamentally possible. He seemed in earnest and they definitely weren't the most bonkers things he had ever said. Those were, in order: "It's a spade, happy fortieth birthday;" "Don't worry, it's only a toe;" and "Why don't you just wear my trousers then?"

But no, the morphine had begun its work and started to chip away at his world.

It's a slow process, getting older. You don't notice. Maybe you do at first, especially if you're used to travelling a lot. Perhaps you notice the last long-haul stamp in your passport and think – that was five years ago now. Then, instead of lengthy drives around Europe and overland tours in Canada, a week in France in a *gîte* seems a bit more manageable. Later, there are weekends in the Lake District and day trips to Whitby and then, eventually, not many of those either. You spend most of the time in your garden. Your world shrinks. Forty-seven countries never becomes forty-eight, but – you think – that's all right, there's always next week, next year.

Is that what it's like, getting old, for someone whose life was in travel? Does it gradually become less important to see new places? Is the garden enough? Do you finally let go of forty-eight?

Is it easier if you have a home – if you come *from* somewhere, rather than always looking *for* somewhere? Is it better if you have a house in a valley under a hill, where you've always lived, where you can go home to when all your travelling is done?

Dad's world finally shrunk to a bed in a ward. Even his last trip – what sounded like a lovely night out at the theatre, thank you doctor – never came to pass.

He lay there, tired from the talking, and I stood at the window again, looking across at the stone tower on the hill that I'd pushed my bike up to a thousand times when I was a kid.

Later, he curled to one side and drew his arms to his chest. A drip ran to one hand and a thin nosepiece delivered air that he took in slow, tentative breaths. The hours passed and his breathing became more ragged, the silences between breaths more pronounced. He never moved, but behind his closed eyes, after one last stonking, morphine-infused, umbrella-adorned cocktail he was surely walking on a beach with a child in each hand, his wife beside him, enjoying the sun but looking forward to going home. At least, I hoped so.

When the nurse came in, she said "Yes, he has," and gently removed the tubes and peeled back the tape from his hand.

"I'm going to just move you down a bit Ken, make you more comfortable," she said, cradling his head while shifting the pillows. "There you are, that's better."

Left alone with him one last time, I held his hands in mine and tracked the folds in his skin around his knuckles. I've now got the same sun-pocked blemishes on my hands that he had on his, legacy of a life in the sun, of a life well-travelled. I'm like him in so many ways, but here – at the end – he was at least within sight of home and I wasn't. I'm not sure what I thought about that.

Anyway. "Bye Dad. See you soon."

Dad had something he would say, every time he bought something new and showed it to you – it didn't matter what, a shirt, a hammer, a car.

"It'll see me out," he'd say, meaning that the shirt, hammer or car would last longer than he would, that it would be the last such shirt, hammer or car that he would ever buy.

It was a joke – partly born of his reputation for being careful, for never throwing anything away, for holding on to something beyond all possible reason because "it might come in handy." It was also a joke because, let's be clear, he said this about anything he ever bought from the age of fifty onwards.

We joined in the joke, because it was ridiculous. The very idea! That that shirt would be the last one he bought. That hammer. That car.

The joke was on Dad, by the way, because that Honda Jazz was *so* the last car he ever bought.

He chose Huddersfield, or maybe Huddersfield chose him, with that job in technical education, with travel as an added bonus, that became his life. He saw something there – a home – that I've never yet seen in any of the places I've fetched up. He leaned into it and raised a family; he made friends and had a life. He filled a garage full of things that would come in handy. He kept going away and coming back home. Forty-seven countries, forty-eight years.

"It'll see me out."

Well, in the end, it's true, Huddersfield did.

And I think he would be happy about that.

From the author

THANKS SO MUCH for reading my book – I know there's lots of choice out there and I'm just delighted that I could share some of my travels and experiences with you.

If you'd like to grab a free eBook while you're here, and travel for a bit longer in my company, then please do sign up for my Takoradi Travel Club. You'll get a free, no-obligation download of *The Travel Writer Chronicles*, containing exclusive tales and tips for aspiring travel writers.

Just head over to my website, julestoldme.com, to find out more.

Did you like this book?

WELL OF COURSE, I hope you did! But as an author, there's no real way for me to tell if you enjoyed reading my book, unless you take a minute to leave a rating or a review.

Why is this important? I thought I'd take a minute myself to explain what a huge difference it makes, especially to independent authors, when kind readers leave a rating or review about a book they've read.

Firstly, I get to hear directly how much you liked the book. It's a thrill when anyone buys my work, and I get another buzz when I hear how you felt about my writing and my travel experiences. Mostly, I just sit here, writing stories and sending them out into the world. It's great when they bounce back from a reader with some feedback, whatever that might be.

The other reason is that, of course, I'd like as many people as possible to read my books. Ratings and reviews really help with publicising my books to a wider audience. In fact, after buying and reading a book, the single best thing you can do to help an author whose work you like is to leave them a review.

So, many thanks in advance, and happy travels!

Other books by Jules Brown

Don't Eat the Puffin: Tales From a Travel Writer's Life

It's the job of his dreams. Get paid to travel and write about it. Only no one told Jules that it would mean eating oily seabirds, repeatedly falling off a husky sled, getting stranded on a Mediterranean island, and crash-landing in Iran.

The exotic destinations come thick and fast – Hong Kong, Hawaii, Huddersfield – as Jules navigates what it means to be a travel writer in a world with endless surprises up its sleeve.

Not Cool: Europe by Train in a Heatwave

Inspired by the budget InterRail trips of his youth, Jules thought he'd try and visit nine cities in nine countries in nine days. Sadly, that wasn't his only mistake.

A tale of relaxing train rides to famous tourist destinations and guidebook sights? Not so much. All aboard for an offbeat travel adventure with a very funny writer seriously in danger of losing his cool.

Find out more

IF YOU ENJOYED this book, here's how to find out more about my upcoming books, projects, trips and events.

Join in at Jules Told Me!

I blog about travel and travel-writing at julestoldme.com, and I'd love to see you there! There are features on over thirty countries on the blog, plus posts about life as a travel writer and how to self-publish. Follow the blog and sign up for the newsletter and you'll be the first to learn about new posts, books and travels.

Books by Trust-Me Travel

Trust-Me Travel is the name of my book publishing company – you'll find it at trustmetravel.com. As well as travel memoirs and adventures, I write and publish travel guides with a twist and how-to guides for travel writers. I'm always happy to consider offers, suggestions and ideas for new books, projects or collaborations.

Printed in Great Britain
by Amazon

84027708R00119